Religion? What's the point?

The power of positive thinking is undeniable. With the popularity over the last four decades of such methodologies as *The Secret, Creative Visualizations,* and motivational gurus such as Anthony Robbins, it's obvious that Americans have been seeking answers to the complicated problems of every day living where religion alone seems inadequate. So what is the point of religion anyway? Some of these "secondary channels" of spirituality go out of their way to make certain you do not confuse them with any religiosity. What void do they leave behind and is any happiness derived from them truly sustainable? Are religions even meant to help us solve our daily problems or just hopeful portals to some blissful afterlife?

No person should deny themselves their birthright to a life that is completely fulfilled both spiritually and materially. In order to do that, we cannot cut short the continued process of humankind's spiritual evolution. We may not even recognize that there is such an evolution. But unless we do, we will allow science to evolve on its own without the spiritual harmony necessary to avoid self destruction.

Human beings of the 21st Century and beyond are in need of religion that does not conflict with science, is easily accessible to anyone regardless of social stature and education, and while helping one to fulfill the needs of modern living has the ability to answer the great mysteries of life, death and human purpose.

Confessions
of an
American
Buddhist

Confessions of an American Buddhist

Written by
Michael Steven Friedman

"Youth, and indeed life itself, flash by in the blink of an eye. That is why it is important for you to ask yourselves what you can do for those who are suffering, what you can do to resolve the mournful contradictions that plague society, and boldly take on these great challenges without shunning the problems and difficulties you will inevitably face."

Daisaku Ikeda
President, Soka Gakkai International and founder,
Soka University of America, Aliso Viejo, CA

All photography by Carl Jackson

*Special thanks to Marion Bradley, Amy Caterina, and
Anastasia Cassell-Young for their time and kind
encouragement.*

First edition release, October 2, 2007

Printed in the United States of America.

ISBN: 978-0-6151-8033-5

For more information, post a review, or to order more
copies, please visit:

www.confessionsofanamericanbuddhist.com

Confessions of an American Buddhist

Table of Contents

Prologue

From Beyond

S itting in my office on that Monday became unbearable as the cold ailment that came upon me on Saturday night was now in full swing. Normally I can work through most common colds, but this was cranking itself over my tolerance level. I began to tag this as the worst cold I ever had. And while that may or may not be true, one thing was certain; the office became unbearable and bed became my only option.

While I somehow managed to fall asleep that night, my sickness was only getting progressively worse. Normally even with a bad cold, I can usually keep myself in bed especially with a good swig of Nyquil. But some time in the middle of the night I woke up and couldn't bear to stay in bed any longer.

Because of being awake at some ridiculous time in combination with my symptoms, I couldn't say exactly what time it was when I was startled by the ringing phone. *Who the hell would be calling at this time of the night* I thought as I was sitting on the sofa watching TV, drinking some tea? At first I didn't want to answer, but also didn't want the ringing to wake everyone else up in the house. My night was already ruined. Why ruin everybody else's?

As I got up from the couch, I hesitated in answering it. But what if it was an emergency? After all, I have elderly parents that live about 10 miles away. I have two sisters with their families. But the caller ID said "Blocked ID." I felt relieved to see that it could not have been my parents or sisters who don't have their phone numbers blocked. So who was calling at this ungodly hour in the morning? Could it be some stupid kid calling the wrong number after having too much to drink?

I had only a few more moments, a few more rings before the answering machine would pick it up. But I began to feel a chilling need to answer. I remember the hairs standing up on my arms. When I finally pushed the talk button I could only answer with a soft voice instead of any sort of anger. But no one replied. I asked several times; *"hello?"* There was only silence. Something felt so bizarre about this call. Perhaps anyone would have an eerie feeling about getting a call in the middle of the night, but something was different about this call.

At about 3:00 or 4:00 AM, I decided to head back to bed. There was no way to tell if I was going to manage getting back to sleep, but I knew I needed to try.

Just before 6:00 AM on that Tuesday morning, the phone rang again. Normally I might not have been able to hear it, but the bedroom door had been left open. Although it woke me up with only about 3 hours of sleep, I assumed it would be my wife's employer who often called early in the morning if she were needed. Unfortunately, she had walked into the bathroom and could not hear it either. So it just kept ringing until the answering machine probably picked it up downstairs. But not more than five minutes after it stopped, it started ringing again. This time I yelled for her to please run down and answer the phone. She hurriedly ran downstairs to pick it up.

I was feeling like crap as I laid there staring up at the ceiling. But suddenly a thought came over me. *My wife was going to come back upstairs and tell me that my father died.* Why would I think that? It's true that my dad was not in the best of health, but at 77 he was still working part-time as an elementary school crossing guard and it wasn't as though we were on some sort of death watch as he laid in a hospital bed. He wasn't even sick.

But here she was walking into the room fighting back tears, "Honey, your father died last night."

I mumbled back to her, almost numb and without feeling, "I knew you were going to tell me that." Why would that thought have occurred to me?

I called my mother immediately.

In spite of how sick I felt, I made it over to my parent's Huntington Beach home from where we lived in Santa Ana, CA in about 45 minutes from the time I spoke to my mom. My sister Debbie and her husband Bill were already there and my mother was sitting across the kitchen table from the coroner who was just about finished wrapping things up. After some hugs and exchanging of sympathies, I briefly had a chance to speak to the coroner. She told me my father died at around 1:00 AM but my mother didn't discover him until just after 5:30 AM (where he had died in the bathroom) after noticing he had never returned to bed.

In the two days that followed up until the funeral, my illness got progressively worse. In addition to the cold, I started getting bronchitis and then both of my eyes became so infected I could hardly keep them open. I was a horrid mess.

It was during these days leading up to the funeral that I began thinking about that extremely unusual phone call that occurred in the middle of the night my father had died. As I mentioned I was somewhat delirious from the sickness and had no idea what time the call actually came in. But an unnerving thought occurred to me; *was it my father?* Once again, my parents don't have their caller ID blocked and in addition my father died in the bathroom with no phone nearby.

I began playing the feeling of that call back in my mind; the shock of the ring, the hesitation to answer... the eerie silence on the other end. Why on the night my father died did that happen? Why was I awake to answer it? And most importantly what time *did* that call come in?

It was easy enough to research the call since at the time our phone service was provided by the Vonage internet phone company. All incoming and outgoing calls can be viewed on the web instantly. So I logged into my account and looked for a call that came in some time after midnight on March 14, 2006. As I anticipated, the caller ID was listed as "blocked." But it was the time the call came in that stunned me. I answered it at 1:01 AM on March 14, 2006; the very time the coroner determined his time of death!

I went and sat in front of our family Buddhist altar and began chanting *Nam-myoho-renge-kyo* which is the mainstay of our Buddhist practice and our form of prayer. A rush of emotions began to overwhelm me. My father had reached out to me. Not from this life but from the moment just beyond. I was certain of it. Why me? What was he trying to say? What *did* he say? As I continued chanting, the answers started flowing in. I have no way to describe it except to perhaps compare it to the film '*Close Encounters of the Third Kind'* where the main characters are given a message from alien beings but not through any visuals, speech, or text. Rather, the message relayed to them was somehow placed into their subconscious mind that they had to bring forth. The silence on the other end of the phone that night was no longer silent at all.

As I continued to chant, the first "message" I felt was the warm calming feel of death. My father was telling me that I should have nothing to fear and that my feelings about death were correct all along. Life *does* in fact continue and I should let everyone know that it was OK. I felt a deep apology from him to the little boy that was his son for perhaps not being the father he would have liked to have been as a young man and I began to cry almost uncontrollably. He was telling me that I could reach him through this period of death through my Buddhist practice and asked me to continue in helping him change his destiny during his transition between lives. I pledged to him that I would.

This book is dedicated to my father, Raymond H. Friedman because his death gave me the inspiration to share this Buddhism with my fellow Americans as well as my mom Stella without whose constant support I could not have achieved much of anything. Common parents who lived a very modest life since they only had the most modest means to do so. I have no PHD in religion (including Buddhism) that qualifies me with any sort of credentials to speak as an academia on matters of religion. I am not an ordained priest that might cause you to respect me more simply because I would dawn a robe. While I work with Buddhist concepts, this book is not intended for the Buddhist student looking to understand deep Buddhist theory weighted in terminology and history.

As will become evident through my story, I am just a person who like most of you has struggled through both good times and bad times within the realm of real everyday life in America. I make no effort to hide the fact that I have made mistakes and have paid for those mistakes. My feelings and thoughts are that of my own. My experience is that of my own. I speak for no organization or anyone other than myself. I don't pretend to think that I have all the answers. I am here simply to share my adventures and confess my heartfelt conclusions after more than 30 years as an American Buddhist.

Chapter 1

From the Night a Long Journey Begins

Stoned on weed and roaming the snow-covered streets of Mayfield Heights, Ohio in my dad's car, Gary and I seemed to have little to do and nowhere to go. It was a snow blown November night in 1975 riding along the familiar streets of this small outlaying suburb of Cleveland where I had spent the first 18 years of my life. Now at 21 and having dropped out of college after three years, I found myself once again living with my parents and completely uncertain of my future.

Hard to imagine that a focused and ambitious kid like myself who seemed to know exactly where he was going could find himself working as a clerk at a camera shop just a couple doors down from the women's shoe store his dad managed for some 15 years. Since 10th grade I had decided to choose a career in the entertainment industry. That led me to becoming a broadcast major at the University of Cincinnati where my two major accomplishments was being the youngest ever elected General Director of the college radio station in my sophomore year as well as one of a very few select students to ever land a job with the ABC Radio Network in New York City as a summer vacation relief engineer.

My summer stint however was not particularly fulfilling as I imagined myself as being one of the worst engineers they ever hired.

My pursuit of the position which began in 1973, finally paid off after driving to New York from Cincinnati financed on a can of coins just to pursue an interview without any guarantee that I would get the job. But what I couldn't anticipate was how inadequate I felt once I started working. Here I was going from just a small closed circuit on-campus college radio station to the big leagues without any local station experience in between. While I was somewhat comfortable with the whole New York City scene after having spent my first summer in Brooklyn right after high school graduation (working for my uncle's burglar alarm company), being in the milieu of one of the three major networks completely freaked me out. What was I doing there? Instead of pushing buttons on a control board heard by perhaps 30 students at a time (who probably weren't even paying any attention), I was pushing buttons that controlled what 3 million people would be listening to.

My nerves were frayed as I made one mistake after another. I played commercials where news sound bites were suppose to go and vise versa or played sound bites from one story that belonged to another. I often jumped cues and played sound bites or commercials while the news anchors were still reading their stories resulting in double sometimes even triple audio. Or even worse, fumbling with buttons on the control board not certain what to do resulting in the two most horrid words in broadcasting, DEAD AIR! If they were looking to hire someone to create the greatest blooper reel of all time, they certainly hired the right guy!

Each time I made a mistake a trouble report had to be written up and served to my supervisor, Harry Curtis. Having a copy for myself after each incident, I ended up with a locker full of them by the end of that summer. With that, I figured going back to the city that I had fallen in love with and even my dream of transferring to a college in New York City were pretty much dead. At the same time I also lost any desire of graduating from the University of Cincinnati and even with only one year left, I dropped out and moved home to Mayfield Heights.

~~~

Because of the heavy snow, very few cars were out that night as we traveled along volumes of a child's history known only to me. Once at the very outskirts of Cleveland's suburbs, Mayfield Heights changed with each year. Like the fading memories of my own childhood, brighter lights from larger and newer stores were dimming the things I once knew. Although I found a few icons of my childhood still remaining along Mayfield Road like Harry's Liquor Store where kids used to ride their bikes to fill small paper bags of penny and nickel candy, much had changed. About 50 yards from the house I grew up in and across a dirt road that rarely saw cars, stood a dense wooded area that we simply dubbed "the woods." I'm sure the developers never knew how traumatized a small group of boys were to see their haven of imagination, with its ponds of tadpoles, running creeks, and wild blackberry vines, torn down and replaced by houses and streets. Ridgeberry Road was now paved, crowded with speeding traffic, and no longer an easy cross-over for a seven year old on his bicycle.

~~~

As the call of munchies brought our pointless night into alert purpose, there beyond the desert of swirling snow, Gary and I spotted an oasis of culinary stoned head bliss; Kentucky Fried Chicken.

As we entered this establishment (whose familiar smell even to this day takes me back to watching the Cleveland Browns on Sunday afternoons with family and friends), we appeared to be the only folks in Mayfield in need of a late night greasy chicken snack. A beautiful young woman stood behind the counter as we approached to place our order. I couldn't tell if her bright magnetic smile was one of mutual attraction or if she was just immensely thrilled to see a couple of living creatures step in from the cold and break the monotony of this deserted night.

After finding a choice table to keep her in my line of sight, I simply couldn't help peeking over periodically to the tall, thin, attractive blonde standing behind the counter. Gary was talking about something but my mind wouldn't register any of his words as my attention was diverted elsewhere. Besides, he was stoned and probably didn't care anyway. With each of my momentary glances, she seemed to be returning a welcoming smile. *This is a done deal! I am definitely going to get this chic's phone number.* I had not met anyone of the opposite sex since moving back home a couple of months earlier. This girl was hot and seemed to be around my age. What better way to break the doldrums of Mayfield than getting a date?

The tray didn't even touch the front counter before I sprang to my feet happily volunteering to deliver the food to our table. As I approached, I was able to confirm that the mutual smiles were not a figment of my imagination. She *was* really smiling at me. Not that I had any reservations about my looks as I was considered a very good-looking guy at 6 foot 2 inches.

Often met with disbelief that I was Jewish, most women described me as having an all-American look. *No way, you don't look Jewish at all* (whatever *that* means). But probably because I was still shaking off my own self-imposed embarrassing image of a kid who would cower from fights in school and didn't seem to have what it took to be a sport jock, I was still surprised and a little uncertain of myself when a pretty woman showed attention. It wasn't until my junior and senior years when I became popular from starring in high school plays and musicals, that I finally enjoyed anything about public school. Kindergarten on up through tenth grade were confidence buster years when it came to the opposite sex. Even the slouched posture that I was constantly working to correct seemed to be a result of years inflicted with nerd-a-ritus.

~~~

Grasping the tray, I boldly decided to give this young lady one last close encounter smile.

"Michael, don't you recognize me?"

Startled and caught off guard by the fact she knew my name, I could only sort of shake my head one way or the other. *OK, give me a hint.*

"Christy. Christy Canfield."

Holy cow! Christy Canfield?

Christy Canfield was the very first friend I ever had. We met at around the age of 4 after my parents moved to this well kept middle and lower middle income class community. The Canfields' lived a few doors down on the same side of the street. In those days people didn't take a whole lot of time getting to know each other especially when it was discovered you had kids who were the same age as was the case with Christy and me. In spite of only a few vague memories of playing with Barbie and Ken dolls or playing "house," Christy and I were together every day. We were best friends. When Kindergarten started, we somehow landed in the same class. In fact, we would remain in the same class all the way through grade school.

Around the age of six however, my mom became pregnant with my youngest sister, increasing our family from two to three kids (myself being the oldest). After Lynda was born, our small two-bedroom house started becoming a bit *too* small as my sister Debbie and I were sharing our bunk bedded room with a crib and an infant. While my dad didn't make much money working as a shoe salesman, my dad's parents were always willing to help out. In fact I think it was my grandparents, 1920 immigrants from Hungary, who told my mom and dad that we needed to get a bigger house even if they had to put up the down-payment to make it happen.

So they found a three bedroom house and we moved. The walk from the Worton Blvd. house to our new home on Orchard Heights Dr. was just around the corner and probably no more than 150 yards from house to house, but to a couple of six year olds it might as well have been 150 miles. Besides, now I was moving across the street from a boy who was also my age. Oh but not just any boy, a Jewish boy at that. In a community that was less than 3% Jewish, it was a nice find; at least for my mother.

So in came Larry Collins and out went Christy Canfield. And in spite of the fact that Christy and I were still seeing each other in class every day, our friendship slipped behind us. Junior high school became the world of broken elementary cliques. Kids you saw every day for seven long years were now thrown into a new world of "subject" classes and homerooms. It was growing up placed into high gear as we each began finding our identities and our places while the chaos took time to make sense.

As we went through the tumultuous late sixties and on into the early seventies, Christy and I became nothing more than casual acquaintances that might say hello in the school hallways whenever we would pass each other. As we continued to grow into our teen years and on into high school, our choices of peer groups were also quite different as Christy seemed to have swung to the more radical world of hippies.

All along, while I didn't have any real contact with her, our mothers remained good friends and I would often get tidbits of Christy info as it became available. Being a typical self-absorbed teenager, I really wasn't particularly interested. For our moms it probably seemed like only yesterday when I was flexing my 5-year-old biceps in Christy's backyard to demonstrate my manhood as we played husband and wife in our toy kitchen. But to me, it was another lifetime hardly remembered.

~~~

And so now I stood in front of a beautiful young woman whose image didn't match what I would have expected. I had implanted an image of a drug abusive down and out hippy that was probably anorexic and living on the street somewhere or making money selling candles. I recall being told that she moved in with some hippy guy right after high school on Coventry Road, once considered the Greenwich Village of Cleveland in the 60's. A more acceptable concept now, but back then living outside of wedlock was still pretty much taboo especially at such a young age. It wouldn't be until much later that I remembered something much more startling my mother had told me in one of her Christy reports.

After the initial jolt which was probably vocalized by an awkward *wow*, it didn't take long to study her face and come to the realization that I *was* really standing before the very first friend I ever had in this world. Stranger still was the fact that I was about to ask my pre-school buddy for her phone number with the intention of getting a date.

And so the next day on Saturday it didn't take long to give Christy a call.   After talking for a while about what we'd both been up to for the last 15 or so years, I worked up the courage to see if she would want to get together that same evening.

"Tonight?" she asked.

"Well, yeah I thought maybe you might like to see a movie or something."

"I can't," she paused, "I have some people coming over to my place this evening."

"People?" *maybe a party?*

"Well, it's a meeting."

"Meeting? What sort of meeting on a Saturday night?" I asked.

"It's a Buddhist meeting."

Suddenly it struck me. My mother had told me about this a while back!

"Michael, you're never going to believe what Christy Canfield is into now!"

"What's that Mom?"

"She turned Buddhist?"

"Oh really?   Whatever."   And I'm sure I must have thought that she had really gone off the deep end.

I can't be sure if it was simply a desperate desire to get a date coupled with the fact that life had become pretty boring, but without even a pause I immediately asked, "Would it be alright if I came to your meeting?"

"Yeah,   sure,   certainly!"   said   Christy   who sounded not only a bit shocked herself that I would be so open ask, but even seemed excited about my coming over.

In fact after hearing her reaction I was now more than willing to sit through some funky Buddhist meeting if it meant any possibility of getting that date. Besides, Christy looked quite normal when I saw her the night before, even extraordinarily normal considering what I would have expected. Her tall thin body was dressed in regular American girl clothing instead of rags.   The delicate features of her pretty face were adorned with makeup and no parts of her blonde hair appeared to be shaved off. In any case, it seemed like a far more exciting alternative than sitting at home watching TV with my parents or smoking pot with Gary again.

Karmic Strings

Picture the inside of a perfectly square gigantic empty   room,   with   perfectly   planed   walls,   no obstructions of any kind, and with no gravity allowing endless perpetual motion.   Then imagine a perfectly round rubber ball at the very top center point of the room. We then propel the ball downward so precisely that it slowly goes straight to the center of the floor then bounces straight up to the center of the top again. And because there is no gravity to stop it, the ball should continue bouncing forever in a perfect straight line up and down.

Now let's say you were to suddenly strike the ball from the side. We'll call that a *cause*. The ball now moves in a different direction. Each time the ball hits a wall, floor, or ceiling we would call that an *effect* of the *cause* created once we altered the movement of the ball.

With the right scientific tools to measure trajectories, velocity, ball density, or whatever else would be needed, you could accurately calculate from the force and angle of the original *cause* the precise point of contact each and every time the ball strikes from one wall to another.

So let's consider the first 50 strike points. If you were able to freeze the motion at the point of initial impact, you could take a string from the ball and stretch it to strike point number 1. Then from point number 1 you could stretch it to point number 2 then to point number 3 and on and on until you got to contact point number 50 before the ball even moves. So what you would see would be 50 lines that would start at the ball (from the point at which it was struck) and end at point number 50. In a sense this would be similar to what a professional pool player sees before he strikes the cue ball. Through his experience and careful study, he can actually see these "strings" before he even hits the ball. He knows how hard to strike the cue ball, where to strike the cue ball and at what angle (*cause*). Even if it has to bank off a couple of different sides and use another ball, he finally hits his intended target that sends the ball into the intended pocket (*as a series of effects from the initial cause*).

For a very short moment what the pool player is attempting to see is his future. Granted, not every shot goes the way he would like, but the argument would still hold true that even the missed shots would still have a predictable future if we were to study in exact detail how the cue ball was struck even though it did not meet the pool player's intended result.

As with this, we can also retrace any event in our lives as strings of events where one thing leads to another. Had I not stopped at her place of work that night on Mayfield Road, I would not have run into Christy (at least on that night). The moment of that encounter can be traced through a "string of events" all the way back to my birth.

It's so simple it's stupid. The strings of our bouncing balls can be easily traced backwards from where you are sitting or standing reading this book at this very moment all the way back to your own birth. One event led to another, which led to another and so on. *So why not ponder that the strings of our **future** are already laid out*? Isn't it possible (even logical) that my seeing Christy again after all those years was destined to happen long before it ever happened? If we think about our bouncing ball in the room or the pool player's shot, then we can see that one thing *does* in fact lead to another.   This is destiny and in Buddhism what is commonly referred to as *karma.*

If the cue ball hits one bumper, then another, then hits a ball, which hits the intended ball, which finally knocks the intended ball towards the intended pocket, then the plan was fulfilled even if the ball missed.   It's not an accident that the ball fell into the pocket or missed it.   The player planned it that way by the manner in which he hit the ball.

You may argue that there is a difference between a conscious intention and one that is not.   The unplanned intention is what we might label an "accident."   But causes that we make take on their own plan.   Even if the pool player had missed his target, the moment he hit the cue ball he still created destiny albeit not the one he wanted.   In fact the moment he hit the cue ball the destiny of the ball was simultaneously created.   In a sense, the result of the shot already happened.   While we must observe a chain of events as we watch the ball hit one bank, then another, then another ball which hits our intended ball, the destiny or *karma* of that shot happened right at the point of initial impact by the pool player.   Even if he didn't fulfill *his* intentions, it doesn't mean the shot itself didn't meet its *own* intention.   In fact every shot, every *cause* will meet its intention.   This is called the *simultaneity of cause and effect.*   Once again while we must view a chain of events over time, the result already occurred the moment the cause was made.

Therefore, the concept of *karma* abolishes the possibility of luck and happenchance.   They don't exist. So what about being in the wrong place at the wrong time or the opposite? Even if it feels that way, there is no such thing. You are always in the place you are suppose to be in at the time you are *suppose* to be there in every single moment of your life because a cause was made at some point that put you where you are at. *Oh, you might not always like it.* The pool player didn't like the fact that he missed his shot, but he's the one who hit it. He can't blame it on the cue ball. The cue ball did exactly what it was suppose to do. And so right place, right time, doesn't mean good place/good time or bad place/bad time. It just means that every moment was destined to happen from the creation of a cause just like the strike of our bouncing ball that had invisible lines ahead of itself from the very moment it was struck.

What if we were to contemplate an iconic tragedy like the sinking of the *Titanic* for example? How did all these people get on this one doomed ship? The answer can be explained in the concept of *collective karma*. Let's go back into our big 'ole square room with our ball that we whacked and which is bouncing all over the place. Now let's add another ball and let someone else hit it. Then another, and then another until we have hundreds of balls bouncing wildly in our room. The rules don't change. Even as one ball strikes another, even if three, four, or one thousand balls strike each other at the same time, it's because each one of those balls traveled along their own string of destiny part of which was coming together at the same moment. While it all may look random and chaotic, there is nothing random about it. Each cause is still fulfilling its own destiny.

But it's not just people that have karma. It's not even just living things. It's actually everything. Every nut and bolt of the *Titanic*, every wooden plank, every drop of paint, every plate, every chair, and as a whole, the *Titanic* itself had destiny. But you argue; *the Titanic is not living and cannot make causes.* That's true, no it can't. But neither can a cue ball.

The question is, if *karma* exists; if there are strings of destiny that lay before us, is there any way to "see" them and take action to avoid bad situations? The short simple answer would be no, there is no way to avoid them. Once you've set the ball in motion, there is really no way to avoid the effect(s). The much longer answer however is YES, you can see those strings and while you can't avoid the effect entirely, you can *sort of duck* it... for lack of a better way to put it. More importantly you *can* alter your destiny if you know not where to look, but rather *how* to look.

~~~

Christy was living in an apartment that was several adjoining towns west of Mayfield Heights. Even though the drive that night was probably only 10 miles, it quickly turned into a different world as you went from the baby boomer homes built in the fifties and sixties, to the large brick, rock solid porch front houses, and stately Tudor homes that were built before World War II.

The streets were now well plowed as the heavy snow had taken a break from the night before. After parking the car, I entered her apartment building and began to ascend the stairs to her unit. Almost immediately an odd noise could be heard echoing in the stairwell.   It appeared to be the voices of people chanting in unison almost to the point of a hum that I could only assume must be coming from this Buddhist meeting I was making my way to. This seemed to be confirmed as with every step upward, the sound got a little louder. While I began to have second thoughts of continuing my climb, I had to remind myself to keep an open mind. More importantly, once I could get past this Buddhist thing (whatever it was), there was still the prospect of the warm company of a pretty young woman which was certainly one thing that I greatly missed since moving back home.

Standing outside her door while substantiating that the sound was clearly coming from her unit, I looked down and noticed various sized male and female footwear still wet from melting snow. I also seemed to catch the scent of incense coming through the door. Again I debated whether I should knock since I might be intruding on some sort of meditation ritual. I feared my knocking might throw these folks out of whatever dreamy zone they might be in. Maybe I got there too late and should have been there before any of this got started. I already was feeling awkward and imposing but since I already made the drive, parked the car, and climbed the stairs, I figured I would feel worse if I turned back and went home. *Maybe a quiet little knock would show respect and my concern not to be rude.* And so I gently knocked but no one responded. *Okay, well maybe that was too quiet.* So taking a deep breath I decided to strike a bit harder. I waited a few seconds and then heard the door unlatch.

Christy stood there with a big bright smile and as we quickly greeted each other she gestured for me to come inside. Luckily I stepped into a foyer that blocked any sighting of the room where the chanting was coming from. I took off my coat and threw it on top of a pile of other coats. Then after taking off my own shoes, as it seemed to be the custom, I apologized for not having taken them off in the hallway but Christy gestured telling me not to worry about it and to just leave my shoes there.

The room she led me into had about ten people sitting on the floor. Some were sitting cross-legged but most were sitting with their butts on top of their heels, legs folded underneath. It appeared everyone was looking at something inside a finely crafted wooden box sitting on top of an altar that had a pair of lit candles, some fruit, and burning incense. In this box with its doors opened, there hung a scroll of cloth or paper that had Chinese writing scribbled all over it. Sitting down on the floor next to Christy, I looked around and noticed that everyone seemed pretty normal. No shaved or partially shaved heads, no monks, no painted lines down foreheads... just people (most of whom appeared to be in our age group) wearing normal street clothes. The only thing that seemed out-of-place was what they were all doing. All sitting on the floor chanting an odd phrase over and over again to an anomalous scroll in a box with palms together in a prayer fashion while holding some beads. As the two of us took our own floor spot behind everyone at the back of the room, I looked over at

Christy who gave me a smile as she herself began to chant along. I smiled back.

Suddenly, someone in the front of the altar rang a bell which caused everyone to stop chanting. But quickly the bell rang once more and everyone started chanting again, but this time they all appeared to be reciting something from these little books they were all holding. I felt Christy's arm nudge me as she put her own little book between us so that I could apparently follow along. While I had perhaps anticipated a deep philosophical discussion or lecture on Buddhism, instead I found myself sitting on a floor as I amiably followed Christy's finger gliding along lines of Chinese characters that had their phonetic sounds written below them.

After they went through this book several times with more bell ringing and with more chanting, they finally came to an end with everyone saying "thank you" and happily clapping and shouting. Then suddenly a couple of the chanters got up and started leading the group in a vigorous song while flapping their right arms back and forth to the song's rhythm. *At this point I was willing to forget the date and simply get back home.* The song ended with everyone cheering and clapping once more. Suddenly this tall good-looking guy jumps up welcoming everyone and asks Christy to introduce her guest. That of course would be me.

"This is my friend Michael," she replied as everyone again clapped and cheered while turning to me.

"Great Michael. My name is Peter and tonight this meeting is for you!" Followed by more clapping and cheering. Now the question that must have quickly run through my mind was, *hold on a second here, how could you all know that I was even coming? Instead of my self-imposed image of an intruder, I now had been elevated to the guest of honor.*

Standing up in front of the room, a couple of people excitedly gave testimonial type experiences about chanting for a job or for a car. Then a few people stood up and gave various explanations of the Buddhist practice they were indulging in. There was an explanation of the phrase they were chanting over and over again; *Nam-myoho-renge-kyo.*[1] Then a quick explanation of the scroll of paper everyone was chanting to inside the altar called the *Gohonzon* and a brief history of the practice which dated back to 13th century Japan and a Buddhist priest named Nichiren Daishonin. All that time however I was probably more fascinated with what Buddhism had to do with cars and jobs.

Finally the meeting came to an end after an hour with one last song followed by everyone chanting *Nam-myoho-renge-kyo* three times.

As everyone stood up several people came over and introduced themselves including Peter as he stood alongside Christy.

---

[1] Phonetic pronunciations: "a" like in father, "o" like in oat, "e" like the sound of the "a" in ape, "yo" like in yoyo, and "g" is hard as in gate. All phonetically spelled Buddhist words have the similar pronunciations of vowels and consonants as in Spanish.

"So, what did you think?" said Peter with his handsome smile.

"It sounded pretty interesting," I half-wittingly replied.

But before I knew it, and probably because of Peter's good sales technique, I was handing over a $5.00 donation and filling out some sort of form. Since I also began to sense that there was more of a relationship between Christy and Peter that went beyond just being good Buddhist buddies, I figured I might as well leave the impression that my intentions were simply pure friendship rather than anything else. The $5.00 seemed more like a gratuitous donation to their "thing" rather than any actual commitment. I'm not even sure I knew this meant I was going to receive one of these *Gohonzon* scrolls of my own that I could chant to as well.

My head was swimming from the events that had taken place that night, only too glad to finally be done with it all. But as I was saying goodbye to everyone and leaving Christy's apartment, this small Japanese woman grabbed my arm squeezing it as she held me at the door before leaving.

"It not matter if you come back or not," she said. "But please try chanting *Nam-myoho-renge-kyo*. Just try. OK?"

As I paused for a moment and looked in her eyes, I could sense a certain deepness of sincerity in her voice that struck me more than anything I had heard that night. I could only nod my head that I would agree to her wishes. And as I waved one last goodbye to Christy and Peter as they stood side by side in the foyer before closing the door, it was the unaffectedness and genuine warmth of this little Japanese woman I seemed to have carried away with me. While her English was obviously limited, she poured her entire life into that last moment as though it were the last opportunity to tell me something I needed to hear. And even if I had heard nothing else that night or even pondered my inability to ask Christy out on a date, somehow I heard what she told me.

Chapter 2

Finding the Right Side of the Happy Coin

I t was Sunday morning. I had woken from the night before where I had apparently completed an application to become a Buddhist. *An application to become a Buddhist?* How bizarre was *that?* Yet while I had no idea what I had gotten myself into nor had any worries about being taken by force into this fellowship of chanters, I felt a certain excitement about giving this thing a whirl and seeing what might happen. After all, I was told I didn't have to believe in anything and could chant for whatever I wanted. That was easy enough as I didn't have the foggiest idea what I was suppose to believe in anyway. Furthermore, I did not recall anything said that night that would have conflicted with the philosophies of an agnostic Jew. In fact much of it made good common sense.

And so I really couldn't have cared less if this was some sort of voodoo or magic. I was in somewhat of a desperate situation and in an open minded position to at least give it a shot. In limbo living at my parent's home, having lost most of my hope of ever going back to New York City after my botched up summer at ABC News, and having dropped out of college with no clear future ahead of me, I was willing to try nearly anything and this seemed quite harmless.

So there I was sitting at the edge of my bed holding the beads and little sutra book that Christy had given me. I placed my palms together and while just looking at a wall, began clumsily and quietly chanting the phrase, *Nam-myoho-renge-kyo.* I was excited. I don't know why but I was. Perhaps because I felt a certain sense of hope that I had lost. Frankly I can't explain it, but it felt good. Doing something I didn't understand was OK. Again, maybe it's because the belief factor was out of the mix. In a way, it was the curious sensation of taking a ride to a place that had to be better than the one I was currently on which in fact was no ride at all. Worse yet, a ride in the wrong direction because when your life seems to stop moving forward, the one thing that doesn't stop moving is time.

Although my parents, with their deep traditional upbringing, had some reservations about this new thing I was trying, they didn't give me a particularly hard time. In fact my dad helped me whip together a simple wood *butsudan* (the box that houses that *Gohonzon* scroll) for my bedroom where I had spent my childhood and teenage years.   There I set up my own little Buddhist altar.

The Buddhist organization known back then as NSA (Nichiren Shoshu of America), which eventually changed its name to SGI-USA (Soka Gakkai International-USA) in the early 90's, was calling me periodically to participate in other meetings.   It was actually Peter, Christy's boyfriend that was doing all the calling. While I was making a conscious effort to keep them at arms length, if it were not for the fact that I genuinely liked Peter, I probably would have completely shut myself off from doing any other activities or going to any other meetings.   But Peter was persistent and I would occasionally agree to go mainly to learn more about what I was doing.

On yet another cold snowy Sunday evening that following January, I agreed to attend a larger meeting to be held at the NSA community center. Since making it known to Peter that photography was one of my hobbies (in addition to working at a camera shop), I was asked to take pictures for the organization's national newspaper (*The World Tribune*).

The center was in the basement of an office structure on Shaker Road on the far eastern edge of Cleveland right near where my grandparents lived and practically next door to St. Lukes Hospital where I was born.

As I was pulling my dad's car down into the underground parking structure, I inadvertently took a right turn a bit too early.   The result was the gut wrenching sound of the sharp edge of a brick wall digging into the side of the passenger door. It was one of those moments where every nerve in your body is pressing itself to go back in time and undo the moment. Unfortunately this was not to be the case as I inspected the damage. It didn't look good at all.

I went into the meeting, took the pictures and tried my best not to think about the victim sitting in the parking garage that I was going to have to present to my father the next morning.

On Monday before going into work, my dad inspected the damage himself.

"What do you think?" I nervously asked.

"Probably over $500, probably closer to $700," he calmly said.

Now I knew I was going to be responsible for paying it back and $700 was a fortune to me at the time. My dad was also not particularly patient and decided that we would go to the body shop that same morning on our way to work and before dropping my mom off at a card shop she worked at.

I sat in the back seat as I watched my dad approach the body repair guy. I was feeling desperate. The prospect of having to pay back my father a large sum of money was upsetting. In addition, my parents were not rich by any means and would cause a hardship for them as well if they had to fork out the money up front. Even with my mother sitting in the front seat of the car, I decided to begin chanting quietly. My teeth were intensely clenched together as I chanted this *Nam-myoho-renge-kyo* phrase in a quiet whisper while I attempted to read the expressions on my father's face as the two men inspected the damage. He certainly was not smiling and would probably describe his expression as one of concern.

Finally the conversation ended as my dad began coming around to the driver's side. I watched and kept chanting. He opened the door and slid in behind the steering wheel.

What I thought was concern on his face turned out to be confusion, "It's only going to be about $175.00."

Did he say $175.00? I can afford that! "Yes!" I shouted.

My dad continued, "I can't believe it's going to be that cheap."

I laughed and clapped and all I could think of that moment was that *it worked*!

Looking back on that experience, it might seem inconsequential almost laughable. One might look at this objectively and say *big deal*. If it were not my own experience, I would probably say it myself. But in the heat of the moment it felt like I had a victory by experiencing a successful outcome on the first thing I specifically chanted for. Later on as I will share, I had other experiences that were certainly far more momentous and affecting in my life, but this was significant as it was the first experience that kept me motivated to continue.

Like any experience in this practice, one can easily trivialize it by saying that it would have happened anyway. And actually there is no way I can prove that statement to be incorrect. Maybe my father was not an expert in auto body repair and just grossly over estimated how much it should cost. But I had no reason to believe that he was wrong, at least not *that* wrong. However one thing was certainly indisputable and that is the fact that the experience propelled me to keep on chanting. Perhaps I wanted this chanting thing to be true more than anything else. I had no real solutions to my problems and could have easily gotten stuck in a serious rut.

But still, I was not jumping in with both feet. I tried chanting a little bit every morning and every evening and was working on learning how to do the ritual called *Gongyo* which includes reciting that little sutra book. But I was still not really interested in getting involved with the Buddhist organization as I had a *thing* about organized religious groups.

I liked the chanting. It made me feel good. It made me feel hopeful. It made me feel like I might not have to try to figure everything out. However, getting involved with organized religion was just not my cup of tea. While I can be a bit of an eccentric, I can also be a bit of a recluse. Getting involved in groups and group mentality of any kind had always made me feel awkward. And so while I continued to chant, the calls from Peter stopped coming as it became apparent to him that I wasn't going to participate.

As the spring of 1976 approached, life in Mayfield Heights was not quite as boring as before. I started dating a young woman I had known through the Jewish youth organization of B'Nai B'rith while in high school. Cindy was going to the University of Kansas in

Lawrence just outside of Kansas City and was at home on break. Instead of constantly depending on my dad's car for transportation, I was able to purchase a brand new Honda CB360T motorcycle, the first of many motorcycles I would eventually own. And while I wasn't really chanting specifically for any of these things, the one issue that I started focusing on most often while chanting was getting my butt out of Cleveland and back to New York City where I wanted to continue college but if only I could figure out some way to afford it.

So one morning in April, I decided to chant for what I felt was nearly impossible; to get my summer job back at ABC Radio News. Besides chanting for a miracle here, I think what I needed to chant for the most was the courage to even make the call and ask for another chance. After my atrocious summer of 1975, I had to believe that Harry Curtis, the engineering supervisor, would be just too kind not to laugh in my face. At least I hoped for that much.

And so with as much fervor as I could muster up, I chanted and chanted that morning for a positive result. I picked up and dialed the phone. Dorothy, Mr. Curtis's very meek and sweet secretary answered.

"Mr. Curtis's office."

"Hi Dorothy, this is Michael Friedman, how are you?"

"Oh hi Michael I'm fine, how have you been?"

"I've been just great. Is Mr. Curtis around?"

"Hold on Michael, let me see if he's available."

"Thank you Dorothy."

"Oh, you're welcome. Hold on."

As I sat there on hold, I was expecting Dorothy to get back on the line and tell me that he was too busy after which I would be told that *if I was calling to come back this summer that sorry, but all the summer positions were already filled.* I could feel my heart pounding in my ear.

"This is Curtis."

I was stunned and unprepared to actually hear the voice of Harry Curtis pick up the line.

~~~

To me, Mr. Curtis had always represented the gate keeper to a world I felt unworthy and unprepared for. I was just 19 years old when I first met him. Steve, an upper-classman at the University of Cincinnati and my predecessor as General Manager of the college radio station, invited me to come to New York to introduce me to Mr. Curtis. Steve was one of a long line of U. C. broadcasting students who were getting summer stints at the network and I wanted to be next.

I was wide-eyed when I first walked into those time-honored studios on the corner of Broadway and 61st Street just north of Columbus Circle in Manhattan. It was the last remnants of a dying golden age of broadcast journalism mixed in with rapidly growing technologies. Most of the news writers were still men. They were still the hard edged salty types dressed in wrinkled white shirts and loosened ties, rapidly banging away on clunky old typewriters with just the index fingers of each hand while puffing on a cigarette. Many of these guys were the ones who wrote and reported the big stories of the forties, fifties and sixties through World War II, Korea, and Vietnam; through three major assassinations, the civil rights movements, America's social discord, and finally Watergate. I imagined that every great name of ABC news had graced these studios at one time or another.

The place was alive with the sound of reel to reel tapes being played back and forth for editing, writers running news copy into the announcer booths as the "On Air" lights went on and off, voices shouting across the newsroom, the sound of those clunky typewriters, and news wire teletype machines pounding away.

Meeting Harry Curtis made me feel as nervous as an elementary school student with an appointment to meet with the principal of a high school. In his early 60's, he exuded authority with his firm un-joking attitude. But after being exposed to a world that far exceeded my expectations, I became determined to be a part of it even before Steve finally led me into his office.

Although I ended up broken hearted in the spring of 1974 when I was turned down for the job, I re-determined to try once more. A year later I drove from Cincinnati to New York City to meet with Mr. Curtis for a second time. Most all the money I had to my name was in a can filled with change. I'll never forget standing in the lobby of the Ramada Inn on the upper west side of Manhattan counting out $70.00 in coins on the reception counter to pay for the night.

But while I successfully landed the job in the summer of 1975, a union paying job for a guy then just turning 20, I botched it up in a big way. For that entire summer and for whatever reason, I just couldn't calm my nerves and settle down.   I was simply a train wreck nearly every day of the week.   Going straight from WFIB, a closed circuit campus radio station, to one of the "big three" was almost surreal.   When I was in high school plays, I would sometimes have the typical actor's dream of forgetting my lines or walking out on stage in the nude.   At ABC that summer, the nightmares were happening for real.

~~~

"Hi Mr. Curtis, its Michael Friedman.   How are you?"

"I'm fine, what's up with you?"

Figuring to get right to the point instead of clumsily trying to have a social conversation, I just took a deep breath and blurted, "Well, I wanted to find out if I could come back again this summer."

Then there was a moment of silence that felt like an eternity.   I braced myself for the news I had expected Dorothy to deliver; a brush off using an excuse that all the positions were already filled.

"When can you be here?" he asked.

Did I hear that correctly?

"Well, as soon as you need me," I quickly blurted out before the lump in my throat would choke me.

This was followed by another seemingly long moment of silence as I waited for him to figure out who he was talking to. *Wait a minute; did you say this was Michael Friedman?   The guy who set the record for trouble reports last summer?   The guy who probably cost this network thousands of dollars in lost advertising revenue because of all the makeup commercials we had to air? Oh sorry, my mistake, looks like we are all filled up this summer.*

"Can you be here by May 4th?" he asks.

OK now let's see, that's a little over two weeks away. I would have to give up my minimum wage job working at Abby's Camera and Art Supply store at Cedar Center in Euclid, Ohio. I may not even be able to give them a two week notice as I might need some time for myself to get ready. Hmmmmmmmm.

"Of course... absolutely! I'll be there."

"Alright, see you then."

"Thank you very much Mr. Curtis."

"OK, goodbye," he said and then just hung up the phone. *Do I dare call him back and reconfirm? "Oh, Mr. Curtis, this is Michael Friedman once again. You weren't joking or confusing me with someone else by chance, were you?"*

I was on cloud nine. My head was spinning. I was going back to New York City! I immediately ran into my bedroom and started chanting to the *Gohonzon* that I had enshrined. I was giddy. While I couldn't be sure that it had anything to do with this chanting thing, I wasn't about to look for doubt at that moment. The result spoke for itself. I was going to keep doing this chanting thing for sure.

With less then a couple of weeks before having to report back to ABC in New York, I decided to hop on my motorcycle and ride from Cleveland all the way to Kansas City, Missouri to visit Cindy. Not an easy feat on a 360cc motorcycle as I would soon discover through the excruciating pain in my back and buttocks causing me to stop and stretch every 50 to 100 miles. But I felt empowered to do anything, even ride a little motorcycle over 1600 miles round trip that actually started in a wet April snowfall followed by hours and hours of non-stop rain. But with just about 5 days to spare, I made the trip there and back. But perhaps the one moment that made it all worthwhile was when I was sitting in a diner somewhere in the middle of No-Wheres-Ville, Kansas. A radio was playing and a broadcast from ABC Radio Network news came on. I was beaming. I'm going *there*!

The summer of 1976 was a different one indeed. Something unexplainable had changed about me. Instead of ending up with a stack of trouble reports like the previous summer, I had none. Not even a single mistake that entire summer. In fact I was so good and enjoyed myself so much, I started thinking about the possibility of turning ABC into a permanent gig instead of just a summer job. And why not, I was chanting. There was no reason to believe that I wouldn't get this too if I chanted for it. But this time I wanted to hedge my bets a little more by contacting the New York branch of NSA and get more involved with the Buddhist organization.

I had gotten word that NSA was going to participate in the July 4th Bi-Centennial celebration and parade in New York followed by a large national convention of its' own in the city. Although I made it to the parade I had apparently missed the NSA performance and was disappointed as I had hoped I might bump into Christy or Peter. In a way, I was hoping that I would even be able to apologize to Peter for having successfully avoided his efforts in getting me to partake in activities back in Cleveland. I even wanted to report to him that much had changed since I started chanting. I wanted to thank him.

I never ended up seeing either of them, but followed through right after July 4th, 1976 by contacting the NSA community center in New York. They hooked me up with a group in Manhattan and I began going to meetings on a regular basis.

As summer's end approached, I began petitioning Mr. Curtis for a permanent position as an engineer with ABC as I now felt completely worthy of it. More importantly, I was chanting in earnest for it. And since I was doing so, I had no doubts that I would be successful in my quest. So confident in fact, that I went out and started spending money that I really didn't have on such things like a state-of-the art audio system; about the best money could buy. I grew confident and cocky armed with this scroll of paper called a *Gohonzon* that life was now my oyster. The thought of going back to finish college paled in comparison with the opportunity of having a career in broadcasting here and now.

But things did not turn out the way I hoped. These were the mid-seventies and some ten years since President Johnson signed into law a new social experiment called *affirmative action*. ABC, like many other large companies, was required to fulfill certain quotas to bridge gaps of racial inequalities.

Unfortunately, being white and male was not an advantage here and was given my good-bye notice at the end of the summer.

I went into a little bit of a panic. I was pretty low on money and alone. I had no idea how I was going to survive.

A Mind is a Terrible Thing to Trust

"The most dreadful things in the world are the pain of fire, the flashing of swords, and the shadow of death. Even horses and cattle fear being killed; no wonder human beings are afraid of death. Even a leper clings to life; how much more so a healthy person?" [2]

Every living creature fights to live no matter how intelligent. An ant for example, does not have the capacity to consider what it knows nothing about yet runs when it is threatened. We humans are conscious of the unknown and like the ant we also have an instinctive reaction to the threat of death. So it's not just fear of the unknown that creates our trepidations with death. Rather, it would appear that the brains' first and foremost purpose is to protect the organism that supports it. But aside from death and upon further examination, we find that our minds (not us) control a lot more than we think.

-----

[2] The Major Writings of Nichiren Daishonin, Vol. I, page 301 (Letter from Sado)

"...one should become the master of one's mind rather than let one's mind master oneself." [3]

The idea seems strange when we consider that our minds may not be in our control. For one thing who is *our*? And while we can easily use obvious examples of psychosis syndromes like addictions or phobias, what about the simple process of everyday decision making?

Let's go back to our brain's inherent function of preserving our existence. There are three basic needs that are relative to this objective and which the brain of all living creatures will fight to protect: consumption of nutrients (food and water), shelter (or any environment that can support life), and sex (for the purpose of reproducing the species). None of these desires have to be intellectualized. Take any one of these three away and any species will cease to exist.

But humans are much different because we have the ability to greatly expand on those three basic desires. We can eat and drink for pleasure, have sex for pleasure, and shelter ourselves with abundant material possessions. We certainly don't settle for fulfilling basic needs for their basic reasons like other creatures. And this is because there is yet another difference that we humans possess as a requirement over other creatures. So important in fact, it became the philosophical theme of our nation as stated in the Declaration of Independence; life, liberty and the *pursuit of happiness*. However that being said, in a 2003 study of the

---

[3] The Major Writings of Nichiren Daishonin, Vol. I, page 389 (Letter to Gijo-bo)

"happiest" people in the world, Nigeria and Mexico ranked 1st and 2nd respectively while the United States of America, the richest and most powerful country in the world, ranked a distant 16 out of 65.[4]   Our constitutional guarantee of this pursuit is not matching up with the success rate in finding it.

Happiness is often measured through comparative perception.   Depending on culture and society we will assume that the person who has the most must be the happiest.   And while it's better to have than to have not, we run the danger of having a distorted set of values.   We end up in "proportionate" happiness thinking it must be better for someone who has more than we do.

While our brains function to naturally give us the three basics, our distinctive *human* desire is happiness. You can argue that a dog seems pretty happy when you hold up a doggy bone.   We also experience similar sensations when walking through a grocery store when hungry or catch the scent of one of our favorite foods as we drive past a restaurant.   The dog was happy when he saw the bone, and we feel happy too when we satisfy our yearning for something like a donut.   But is there any possibility that the dog would feel guilty after eating the bone?   I don't think so.

Very often you may find yourself at odds with your own desires.   In the end, will getting *this or that* make me happy or won't it?

---

[4] New Scientist Magazine (United Kingdom)

We all spend our days going through a series of desires; from getting up in the morning, to brushing our teeth, to getting to work, to eating dinner, to watching television, to getting back to bed... and then starting the whole thing all over again. Looking at it this simply it can appear to be a pretty sad existence, but the fact remains that just about everything we do can be connected to some sort of desire or another.

Happiness: Humankind's Fourth Basic Desire

While I felt shattered when I failed to get the job at ABC News, I could not at the time know if attaining that job would have contributed to my happiness. In the short run perhaps, but how could I know? I was reacting to the environment.

Since birth, we are trained into believing that happiness comes from getting what we want. In turn we associate unhappiness with *not* getting what we want or losing things we have. To have or not to have... that is the question; the two opposite sides of our happy coin. And while everyone has their own levels of what they feel they need to live happy lives, we still have to make a myriad of choices throughout. *What career should I choose? Whom shall I marry? Which car should I buy? Should I choose red or white? When shall I marry? Should I buy this? Can I afford that? Should I turn left? Should I turn right? Who should I ask to the prom? Should I invest in mutual funds or stocks? Should I stay or should I go? Is eating that donut really a good idea?* From the tiniest choices to the big life altering ones, the aim is always the same; what will make me happy? What will bring about the greatest pleasure or what will help me avoid the greatest pain? In both cases, they are related to happiness.

While it may be true, that a human being can sustain life with the three basic needs and yet live a life of misery, humanity as a whole has no purpose void of the pursuit of happiness. Our species would cease to exist without this motivation and therefore becomes the *fourth* fundamental need for a human being.

So is it possible then that the human mind also seeks happiness in order to sustain the species just as it does the other three basics? It feels good to eat, good to be sheltered, and good to experience sex. If pleasure or avoidance of displeasure were not associated with all three, we wouldn't care to have any of them. The pleasure seeking mind keeps us alive but at the same time can also misguide us.

While joy may be joy, there are various depths and profundities of happiness just as there are various depths and profundities of love; just as there are degrees and depths of anger and hate. In order to understand this, we must first make a distinction regarding how happiness comes about and understand that there are two kinds: one that needs an outside source to bring it about and maintain it and another that comes completely from within and is indestructible. The first relies upon fulfilling desires but which also carries the consequences of unhappiness when we lose any of those things or fail to obtain them, and the other that we cannot lose since it had no attachments to begin with.

But is there actually such a thing? I believe that every human being yearns for such happiness and the means in which to achieve that state, but for the most part probably don't even realize they are capable of it. In fact, we may not even be aware that it exists. For if the only happiness we can have is based upon our ability to fulfill desires, then the opposite must also be true. In the end we become slaves as well as potential victims of our desires. How can we *just* be happy without relying only on material fulfillment and reliance upon our external world? In fact if we could find such happiness, then it would make any worldly possessions that much more enjoyable, wouldn't it?   Not having to rely on them for happiness but just enjoying them for what they are?

What would be defined as a material desire or "worldly possession" and that which becomes the motivation for making most of our choices? It's not just jobs, cars, houses, and toys. It's *anything* that requires a physical consequence to bring it about and I believe that there are three general categories of material desires: health, relationships to other living beings, and possession of non-living materials. From the suckling of our mother's milk, we graduate to the quality of relationships with our friends and family, the effect of foods we consume, and sometimes cars and boats. Even *time* can be categorized as a non-living possession and therefore a material desire.

Imagine if you could actually have your future read? The main reason we might want to have it revealed is so that we could be certain if we are making the right decisions. We get married, have children, go to college, pick careers, make friends, get jobs, move to new locations, etc. Even the most ordinary decisions like turning down a street might be the difference between life and death. And while we may possess certain gut feelings about our choices (and hopefully more often than not make the right ones), we are never really certain where it will all lead. The classic adage, *only time will tell*, is pretty much the way we live. Pretty much the way we believe we *have* to live. We keep smacking that bouncing ball in a direction we think will make us happy but in the end we have little idea which way the ball will bounce from that point.

But remember once again that for every cause there is going to be a predictable effect. We just don't have the power to see it with our minds. And here is where the mind alone falls short of being able to lead us to happiness. Our minds are geared towards fulfilling those four basic needs: nutrition, sex, shelter, and happiness. The brain is an organ that among other things, functions to preserve our existence. But we know that we are often at odds with what we want versus what we need. And perhaps this is the most important statement I can make regarding happiness: *while we may have no problem knowing what we want, we have little idea knowing what we actually **need** to find the indestructible happiness that I am referring to.* As such, we are led by our mind which only has the capability of seeing what is here and now. We are limited to working from successful stimuli we have experienced in the past.

What is a *gut* feeling? We've all experienced when there is a sense of something beyond our mind that compels us in making certain decisions. There are those who think it's even a source outside our lives that talk to us like God for example. But we constantly cut ourselves short of our own inherent ability to become the captains of our own destiny. We may even think something outside of ourselves is needed to bring about the necessary changes and conditions to create all the right choices since we can never be certain in the end what those are.

The concept of happiness derived from a state inherent from within is the basis of Buddhism. The word *enlightenment* implies a state both abstract and non-figurative. It is a state of happiness that is generated by one becoming conscious of his or her humanity. And what does *that* mean? Infinite in its nature, it involves the realization of the true aspects of life and death, a sense of being, the nature of causality and one's own power to control it, complete satisfaction and the reality of *dependent origination* (discussed later). And if I might borrow a worn-out analogy used in sales, enlightenment is the steak while the things that happen along the way are just the sizzle. As I would discover over the years to follow, this is *the* benefit of Buddhist practice.

Chapter 3:

Death Comes to Life

L uckily, unemployment came to my rescue as I began to explore the main reason I had returned to New York which was to finish college and entered the fall semester as a sophomore at the School of Visual Arts on 23rd Street in Manhattan with a major in film. With the help of my friend Marcia, a young woman I had met 3 years earlier in Brooklyn, NY right after graduating from high school, I found a decent and affordable apartment in the basement of a three story triplex (four-plex if you count the basement), in Jackson Heights, Queens.

All in all, I had felt that although I was denied a full time position at ABC news, I was very much protected by the fact that I could go to school and not even worry all that much about whether I could find another job right away.

~~~

Not long after starting school, I received an urgent call from my sister Debbie. She reported that our cousin had her baby, but with serious complications. Shirley was one of our closest cousins growing up together in Cleveland.

"I don't know. The doctors are saying the baby won't make it through the night," she said sadly. To us this baby was significant as it was the first to be born to our generation from our close knit family.

"What happened?" I asked.

"I really don't know. I feel so bad for Shirley. God, I really don't know." Then half heartedly and with a slight mumbling chuckle she says, "Maybe you can do something with your Buddhist *thing*, I don't know."

I couldn't believe she said that. Maybe *she* couldn't believe she said that. In fact, both of my sisters were very perturbed that I began practicing Buddhism. Later she would tell me she regretted the call. But after all, these were the times following the days of Charles Manson, Sung Myung Moon, and the Hare Krishna's. Some of these cults allegedly kidnapped you, made you sell flowers in airports, and forced you to forget about your non-believing family. So I'm sure it was more the times and their concern about what might happen to me.

It has always been so interesting how we can be against something we know nothing about even to the point of resenting or even hating it. My parents were not happy either but certainly would have even been more distraught had I converted to Christianity. At least with Buddhism, they realized that if they were going to be against it, what exactly were they against? So they just tolerated it as something weird (although my father was a bit more opened minded than my mother and sisters). Maybe they even thought it would be a phase that would quickly die rather than a commitment that has lasted for over 30 years.

I don't want this to sound wrong, but I was somewhat excited after getting off the phone with my sister. While still very new to Buddhism, I felt I finally would have an opportunity to prove the validity of this practice to my family. I called my mom in Ohio.

"Hey mom, Debbie just called me about Shirley's baby."

"Oh Michael, yoiy yoiy yoiy," she said followed by a sort of tis tis tis sound. "Oh my God I don't know, I feel so bad for Shirley. I don't know what to do."

"What did the doctors say?"

"They said the baby won't make it through the night," she replied.

"Are they sure?" I asked.

"Well it wasn't just one doctor. They said the baby is not going to make it. The family is so broken up about this. I feel so bad."

I took a deep breath and said, "Mom, the baby is going to make it."

"Really, how do you know that?"

"Because," and I couldn't believe I was about to say this but I did, "I'm going to chant for the baby and the baby is going to make it."

After a short pause my mom replied with a slight chuckle, "You are going to chant for the baby?" Then offering a little seriousness, "Hey if you think that will work, go right ahead my son."

After finishing the conversation and hanging up the phone, the next thing I decided to do was call my cousin Shirley. This was the gutsiest thing I had ever done in my young life.

~~~

My father's parents had no problem entering the United States from Hungary just after World War I via Ellis Island. For my mother's parents and their first infant it was a much different story. When attempting to enter this country in the 1920's, they were turned away as the immigration department had run out of visa allotments. So instead they headed to Mexico as did many other European Jews at that time.

There after 10 years and 7 more children later my mother Estella was born in Mexico City. But the Great Depression would end up collapsing my grandfather's very successful textile business causing them to migrate to the United States where other family members had already settled years before.

They ended up moving into a rather large duplex home in Cleveland with my grandmother's sister and her children. There, close family ties would grow between my mother and her first cousin Alice Nussenblatt, her husband, and eventually us kids and their three children

Jessica, Shirley, and Eddie.   It actually became a tradition lasting from the late 1950's through the 1970's that no matter what, every Saturday was spent at the Nussenblatts' while every Sunday was spent with my dad's parents. Since my mother's father had died even before I was born and her mother moved down to San Antonio to be with her oldest daughter (and where most of my mom's other brothers and sisters settled), the Nussenblatts' represented the only real family left in Cleveland on my mom's side. Back then air travel was for the rich (or richer) people and even long distance phone calls were special, expensive, and rare. So the Nussenblatts' were given equal family time as they became the only link my mom had to her own blood.

It was clear that Judaism was treated a little differently between the two families. My father's parents were serious about being Jewish but not nearly as serious about the traditions and rituals of Judaism as were the Nussenblatts'. Both sides had strong ties to their European heritage and the plight of the millions of murdered Jews at the hands of the Nazis in the Holocaust of World War II. They themselves lost brothers, sisters, cousins, aunts, uncles, nieces, nephews, and friends. All of this from a time that began some 20 years before I was born and which did not end until the defeat of Nazi Germany. But their pain, their pride, and their loyalties were embedded deep in our family culture.

The Nussenblatts' and my mother, kept strict kosher homes and played into all the Jewish institutions and superstitions that dictated much of how we lived.

On the other hand while keeping appearances at the home of my father's parents Adolph and Margaret Friedman, they were no where near as hard core. For example, my father's mom (whom we lovingly knew as Nana), had one of my favorite treats that I could only get at her home. We referred to it as the mysterious "square meat."

"Michael," Nana would say in her heavily Hungarian/Yiddish accent, "Poppie just went to the grocery store in the machine (which is what she called the car) and picked up some square meat."

Of course she would never actually ask me if I wanted any but instead just served it up. She probably knew the answer would be yes anyway but loved to see her grandchildren eat. I think much of this gratification for many European mothers and grandmothers had to come from their poor backgrounds when starvation was always a possibility. For them, food was more than just nutrition. It symbolized freedom, safety, America, and their exodus from tyranny. As Nana sat there watching her grandchildren eat, I can only imagine the depth of joy she must have felt that came from a place embedded deep within memories carried on by generations before us. It wouldn't be until my later teen years that I would finally realize that "square meat" was actually sliced ham and not at all the kosher kind I might add.

Passover was also split between the two families. The first Seder was held at our house with my father's parents along with his only sibling (Aunt Laura) and her family, while the 2nd night took place at the Nussenblatts'. The first night was the easy night. My father would lead the Passover ceremonies held mostly in English. We started at around 6:00 PM, went to the portion where dinner was served about an hour later, and then called it quits. At the Nussenblatts, while we started at around the same time, the proceedings were mostly in Hebrew and dragged on until dinner (usually around 9:00 PM) and then afterwards continued with the second half of the ceremony that took us nearly until midnight. It was brutal for us kids. However looking back while difficult at times, have never regretted being part of this very rich culture. I suppose if there is anything I can say I regret about having converted to Buddhism is the fact that I no longer carry on traditions that connect me to my ancestors. (It is perhaps difficult to be the first generation of a new culture. But others have felt this way over thousands of years when other individuals first began breaking their own paradigm of religious beliefs.)

This was not the case with the Nussenblatt children who admirably held strongly to the traditions taught to them by their mother Alice. Including Shriley, they still continue to keep strict Jewish homes from what I understand.

~~~

And so when I decided to call Shirley that night to talk to her about chanting for her baby in distress, it was a bolder move than I could have ever depicted myself doing.

For some reason I imagined her standing in her kitchen when I called. She had just come home from the hospital and was choking back tears from the sorrow that was consuming her.

"Shirley, I know you are not going to understand what I'm about to tell you or ask you to do. I've never asked you for anything, but just trust me on this. I promise if you do this your baby will live."

She was either very desperate or too kind to hang up the phone on me but I actually got her to repeat *Nam-myoho-renge-kyo* and even write it down. While I don't know if she actually followed through with my request to try chanting each day, I made a promise to myself that I would sit in front of my *Gohonzon* and chant for 3 straight hours each day for the sake of her baby.

I was certain this Buddhism would work. It had to! This was life and death! It wasn't about a job, a dent in a car, the ability to pay rent, or whether I would catch a subway train on time. It was about whether a little baby would live or die. I felt this was my biggest test.

I'll never forget the intensity as I sat there in front of my altar that very evening after hanging up the phone with Shirley. I was squeezing my palms together so hard as I chanted, I thought I would crush the solid wood prayer beads I was holding between my palms or cause the bones of my arms to break and buckle against each other. I stared at the *Gohonzon* until it actually began glowing and even appeared to float in such a way where I could not see anything else around me. And all the time, my only thought was somehow connecting my life to the life of this nameless baby and make her live.

"Live! Live!" I kept thinking to myself as I chanted.

My neck, face, and entire body would shake from the ferocity of my prayer. Tears welled up in my eyes. I would not be defeated! I would use the energy of my life to encourage this baby to fight for its own. I even screamed while chanting it at times; *"Nam-myoho-renge-kyo! Nam-myoho-renge-kyo! Nam-myoho-renge-kyo!"*

In actuality, I had NO idea what the hell I was doing or what I committed myself to! But I felt I could move the world with my life through this Buddhism without limitation no matter what, whom, or where.

I woke up the next morning and called my mom to get a report on the baby's condition.

"Yep," my mom said. "The baby made it through the night."

"Yes!" I thought to myself.

I went back to the Gohonzon and put in another three straight hours of chanting with the same intensity and same prayer. Another night passed. The baby was still alive. Again back to chanting and again another night passed safely for the baby. For over one week day after day I continued and night after night the baby would get stronger until after what seemed like a little more than a week, the baby with a name (Carrie) went home to her mother and father. I never really spoke about it. I did not go back and throw it in anyone's face or even claim the victory to be mine. I felt good enough after speaking to my mother when she reported Carrie would go home.

"Well son, you must have done something," she said. "The doctors were amazed. Two doctors said they had never seen a baby with that much will to live."

That was more than enough for me. Carrie is now over 30 years of age and whom I finally met for the first time at a family wedding near San Francisco in 2006. I had not even seen my cousin Shirley since I had left Cleveland in 1976. And while Carrie has Down syndrome, I could sense the incredible joy she has brought to her family and how much she is loved not to mention Shirley's own involvement as a teacher herself with children of special needs and the contributions she must have given to her community. Nothing was mentioned about this at the wedding although Shirley was happily curious to approach me and talk a little about Buddhism.

~~~

I began an intimate relationship with my friend Marcia which rapidly grew serious. So serious in fact that she moved in with me. Soon enough we would also become dependent on each other financially; her with a clerical job and me with the small amount of unemployment I was still collecting.

The seemingly irresolute future of two people in their early 20's did not make life easy. Not long afterwards Marcia made it clear that the one thing that would not remain in limbo would be our relationship. In many ways it's hard to blame her, but she needed some sort of solidity to this part of her life and in so many words prepared me for her leaving if I wasn't willing to take it to the next level; marriage. Although she had never come out and said it directly, she more appropriately asked me where I thought the relationship was going or saw no point in remaining in a live-in only situation. More to the point, it was an ultimatum of sorts.

Oh the insecurities of youth! I proposed and shortly thereafter we were married in a Jewish temple with a Jewish ceremony. It all seemed surreal. I cannot forget the day standing up on the synagogue stage in front of the rabbi and Torah. Looking behind me as the music introduced the bride, beautiful in her gown, I could only think in my head the words as expressed by (the not yet famous) Talking Heads; *well, how did I get here?*

Our relationship worsened after we got married. It felt like we were simply arguing all the time about anything and everything. I knew in my heart that this relationship could not last though I certainly had no one to blame except myself.

But after a year of living with each other and about another 6 months of marriage, Marcia reported to me that she was pregnant. We now faced a serious dilemma. Because of my Buddhist practice and beliefs, an abortion was out of the question at least for me. Not because Buddhism itself or the organization takes any official stance in the politics of whether abortion should be legal or not; it doesn't. In fact, I would always support a woman's right to make her own choice and if Marcia had made that choice, I would have accepted it. But it should be left as a personal matter where government has no business. Personally I could not consider abortion as an option especially since we were married.

But in this marriage (that may not have lasted even a year let alone whether it should have happened at all), we were now compelled to make it work since parenthood was up and coming. Still in college about to graduate with no certain future and Marcia in a job void of any real career, these were difficult times for the two of us.

Right after graduating from college in 1979 I was able to land a job as an assistant producer at one of New York's premier advertising agencies, Wells, Rich, and Greene. That at least relieved some of the tension in our relationship, with a steady income, health insurance, and the ability to move out of our basement apartment and up to the first floor two bedroom unit. As the months passed and as we both began focusing on our future child, it seemed things became a bit more civil between us.   Marcia's decision to stop smoking cigarettes once she discovered she was pregnant was certainly a help.

As a child, both of my parents smoked as I lived each day in a smoked filled home driving with my parents in smoked filled cars. Even at an early age I detested the habit to the point where it even became a phobia. I could not even sit near a *clean* ashtray let alone one filled with butts and ashes. Of course I knew that Marcia was a smoker even when I had met her after high school. But having tolerated it through my childhood I was certainly capable and willing to tolerate it temporarily thinking that she would quit once we started living together. In fact she actually tried on several occasions but failed each time. Yet for the sake of the baby, she did manage to stop.

But no matter how poorly our marriage was drudging along, we both fell in love with our unborn baby and looked forward to its arrival.

Coming close to her ninth month and perhaps with only a couple more weeks until her due date, Marcia and I made a weekend trip to Toms River, New Jersey to spend some time with her brother and his family. Being that Teddy was a doctor, we enjoyed the use of his stethoscope to listen to the heartbeat coming from inside Marcia's womb as we watched the baby joyfully kick. Later that same Saturday, we thought we would take it out and give it another listen. But this time I could not find a heart beat. I placed the stethoscope all over but had no luck. Since I wasn't a doctor, I couldn't even know what that meant. Teddy even mentioned the baby may have possibly moved into another position making it more difficult to find. Although we were a bit concerned, we tried not to think about it.

But later that evening Marcia began getting contractions as though she was going into labor. Too far away from home and her own doctor, we had to take her to a local hospital and had a resident obstetrician examine her. I mentioned to the doctor that we had been trying to find the heartbeat with my brother-in-law's stethoscope and while we had heard it earlier that morning, by afternoon we couldn't find it. He also mentioned that the baby may have changed positions which would have made me feel better had it not been for the fact that he was having difficulty finding it himself.

"Well," the doctor said to Marcia and me, "we can't know for sure what this means. The baby may have turned its back or something, but you are definitely going into labor and we will need to keep you here."

I stayed with Marcia in the labor room as the contractions grew more and more intense. Each time the doctor came by to examine her he listened for the heartbeat but still couldn't find anything. I started thinking about Carrie and how I chanted with fiery determination to help will the baby to fight for its life. But now this was *my* baby and while I did not have the opportunity to get in front of my altar, I began chanting deeply inside with the same fervor I had felt for Carrie. I believed with all my heart that because of the many positive causes I was making and all the chanting I had done, the result would be a good one. I could not imagine any disastrous outcome.

Finally after several hours had passed, they decided that Marcia was ready to go into the delivery room. Having gone through all the birthing classes I was certainly prepared to accompany her, but instead the doctor asked me to stay out. Already late into the evening, I found a quiet place in a hospital hallway to begin chanting.

After about two hours a nurse came over to me.

I looked up at her. "Marcia is fine, but your baby didn't make it," she said quite softly and directly. Then after pausing a moment she said, "I'm so sorry."

I was stunned. I was struck emotionless.

"I know this is very difficult and you don't have to if you don't want to, but would you like to see her? The baby I mean?"

"It was a girl?" I asked.

"Yes. I don't think your wife wants to, but if you do we can go."

"Yes," I said immediately. "I want to see her."

Two nurses escorted me to a darkened room. There on a table rolled up was a small white hospital blanket illuminated by a light which I immediately knew must have contained the body of my baby. As the nurse began unwrapping, her body gently rolled over until she was finally facing me. Her eyes were closed as she simply looked like a sleeping, peaceful child. She was beautiful. I could only look for a moment.

While Marcia remained in the hospital for the night, I returned back to my brother-in-law's home and after receiving sympathies from everyone, went to the downstairs guestroom where Marcia and I had been staying.

I could not understand why this happened to us. As a Buddhist it made no sense at the moment. What would I say to anyone about this? Was this proof that Buddhism had no validity? Why should I just accept something like this with no answer? It was unacceptable! Maybe this would be OK for people who practiced other religions, but not this one! Not in this case. I needed an answer! I did not want pacifying words of encouragement. I could not pass it off as the "will" of some omnipotent power outside of myself. The bar that was set for Buddhism was much higher than that. I expected to know something and I needed to know at once! I was willing to put my entire Buddhist practice on the line.

With the bedroom door shut and taking a seat on the floor facing away from the foot of the bed I began chanting with anger. I thought that this could in fact be the last time I would ever chant again. I recalled reading articles and senior members of the NSA lay organization telling me that when it comes to Buddhism, *while we don't always get what we want, we will always get an answer.* Now was that time and this was the night. I was not willing to wait years, months, or even days. I wasn't sure if the tears welling in my eyes were from sadness or my determined anger to have closure and satisfaction. I wasn't even sure how long I chanted but it went very late into the night. I finally decided to lay myself down to sleep.

Placing my head on the pillow I looked up at the ceiling slightly illuminated by the small window above the bed. All was peaceful and quiet as I continued chanting at a slight whisper.

It felt like I had fallen asleep but I couldn't remember falling asleep. I think I was still chanting but I couldn't hear anything or feel my lips moving. I thought I was still looking at the ceiling but I couldn't see it any more. Instead I saw what I thought were clouds moving quickly. Where was I? Then I heard a soft voice. It was the voice of a child.

"Daddy, I'm sorry. But now was not the right time. I will come back."

My eyes quickly opened and I began to sob uncontrollably.

The Death View

"Looking back, I have been studying the Buddha's teachings since I was a boy. And I found myself thinking, 'the life of a human being is fleeting. The exhaled breath never waits for the inhaled one. Even dew before the wind is hardly a sufficient metaphor. It is the way of the world that whether one is wise or foolish, old or young, one never knows what will happen to one from one moment to the next. Therefore I should first of all learn about death, and then about other things.'" [5]

We go through life via a succession of moments from one to the next. You know about your past (at least as much as we can remember of it), you know where you are right now (you are reading this book), and you know there is a future albeit one you can't see. We don't think about getting sick every day when we are healthy yet it would be hard to imagine that at some point we won't catch another cold. It's coming, we just don't know when. No matter how old you are, you are aware that your physical appearance has changed and as much as we would like to stop it in its tracks, we will

[5] The Writings of Nichiren Daishonin, Vol. II, page 759 (The Importance of the Moment of Death)

continue to age and our bodies will continue to show it. It can all get pretty depressing when you consider that the sufferings of life are not a matter of if, but when and how.

I would like to ask you to indulge me in a 30 second exercise. First I want you to become totally conscience of your present moment. Think of your eyes moving back and forth across the page. Consider that your brain is organizing these printed words into thoughts that you understand. Feel whatever you can against your skin like your clothing, the air, this book. There are sounds around you that you hear. Perhaps they are from conversations or a TV coming from another room or passing cars in the street, or crickets in the night. Be completely and totally where you are at this very moment.

Now...

CLOSE YOUR EYES FOR AT LEAST 30 SECONDS BEFORE TURNING TO THE NEXT PAGE. BE TOTALLY CONSCIOUS OF EVERY THING YOU CAN HEAR, FEEL, OR SMELL. BECOME CONSCIOUS OF YOUR THOUGHTS.

You are alive and you are a human being. What is the wonder in that for you? Can you appreciate how profound it all is? No matter who you are, no matter where you are, you are alive. *Alive.*

Now consider this. In all probability you won't remember a thing about the moment that just passed in a few minutes let alone months or years from now. It will be gone. As they say, "lost in cyberspace," perhaps in this case "lost in cerebral space." But more importantly, the eyes that you are reading with, the brain you are sorting and analyzing with, the skin you are feeling with... all of it will be gone in say 50 or certainly 100 years from now. Your physical body will be... no more.

You may not like to hear this and be disheartened at the thought because it is just not something we *want* to think about. Perhaps the most frightening word in the human vocabulary is *impermanence*. Impermanent health. Impermanent age. Impermanent relationships. Impermanent lifetime. It's hard to face up to the fact that everything is temporary. In a sense, everything is an illusion. It exists for just the moment we can perceive it (just like the one you just closed your eyes to be aware of) and which is now gone. In fact we experience the "death" of moments and things constantly. Death/impermanence or the temporary existence of our physical reality is constantly taking place. We may not think about it. We may make a conscious effort *not* to think about it, but in our subconscious mind we are always aware that this moment ends and leads to the next. Today will turn into tomorrow and life will turn to death. The loss of a job, the loss of a loved one, or the loss of health becomes constant reminders of endings. Perhaps even the desire (or fantasy) for riches and fame is deeply rooted in our illusion that death can be cheated by sheltering it even deeper in our mind by substituting our subconscious reality of death with the fantasy derived from worldly possession.

So gloomy is this reality of impermanence, mankind needed religion to create a place of permanence so that the real world could be tolerated. In fact without such a world that might exist in the afterlife, man may surely have ceased to exist since the only permanence would have been nothingness. That sort of thinking is not only depressing, it is also destructive. The idea of such places as heaven and hell became means by which we could tolerate an impermanent existence and fear by our sins another kind of permanence that would leave us permanently suffering.

So as they say in broadcasting, "And now a word from our sponsor. The makers of Common Sense:"

We are all born the same way. It's roughly a nine month gestation period inside the womb of a woman whose egg has been fertilized. No one could survive after 2 months and no one can hang out in their mother's womb for 2 years. We are all born as babies and grow old. None of us are born as old folk and work backwards. We all age. We all get old and we all eventually die. Yet, in spite of all the commonality amongst the world religions like cause and effect ("reap what you sow" for example) and the ideal of brotherhood and caring, they all have their own take on what happens to you when you die. Now I don't know about you, but is it possible that while our entrance and age progression in this life are exactly the same that our exits can be completely different? Most every religion has a "place" to go but common sense tells me that only one can be correct or all of them must be wrong. How could they possibly all be right? Hence we find at least one of the core reasons why religious intolerance has existed for centuries and why millions upon millions have died as a result. Each religion is screwing with the precious subconscious mind of impermanence. If we all believed in the same thing, there would be no problem. We would all agree that we are going to the same place and whether true or not true, there would be no fear of anyone breaching our death levy.

My theory is that religious violence and intolerance over the centuries is deeply rooted in the *death view*. The human mind is so bent on protecting the body and its sanity that it cannot tolerate the thought that whatever one believes in is NOT the path to a blissful *escapist* afterlife existence. It would be best then to destroy someone else's belief so as not to have to face one's own doubts. The thought of impermanence and the need for eternalness work harder on the human psyche than we know because it is a matter of belief rather than factual knowledge. Beliefs can be changed or destroyed. Facts cannot. Animals only exist in the moment. They cannot contemplate past and future. And so, it is one of the great curses of being human. Though all around us and always a possibility at any moment, we give little thought to where death takes us if in fact anywhere. Animals don't anticipate any sort of ending to their lives but humans do. Not only do we think about it occasionally, we think about it subconsciously *all the time.*

Consider when you had planned for a vacation. Whether you were consciously thinking about it or not, once you committed to that trip by spending hundreds or perhaps thousands of dollars for your reservations, didn't you *feel* it in your life 100% of the time? Although you can't know exactly what you would experience, you were totally aware that you were going somewhere, knew exactly where it was, and you prepared yourself accordingly. You weren't purchasing snow boots if you were going to the Bahamas. You weren't brushing up on your French if you were going to Cancun, Mexico and you weren't purchasing snorkeling gear if you were going to see icebergs in Alaska (or what's ever left of them).

In the case of the vacation, while you were "aware" of it all the time, when preparing for it you took specific actions in preparation for the trip. Religions as well offer all kinds of ways to prepare yourself and earn passage to the Promised Land and so you'll try to take those actions as well... as best you can (maybe thinking about it more as you get closer). But once again, we have to go back to fact vs. belief. Your vacation is a fact. What happens to you after you die is not. As humankind continues to evolve scientifically and as the mysteries of the universe that surround us become more fact rather than conjecture, it becomes more and more difficult to buy into the belief that people can rise from the dead, split seas in half, create a complete living planet in six days, etc, etc, or that there is an eternal euphoric dimension like heaven.   The continuous offensive that religions take with science like evolution vs. creationism, can also find its roots in the protection of their *death views*. It's not so much that anyone really cares deeply about whether you can prove the feasibility of crowding the entire planet's living population in pairs of two on a boat built by one person over 4000 years ago. It's where you draw the line between what is literally true and what are fictional parables aimed at teaching righteous principles. For if scriptural tales are proven false, (when for centuries they have been taken so literally to the point of blasphemy if thought otherwise) then the big prize of the *death view* is also threatened. In the end the *death view* is the only thing that really matters. If you could prove by scientific fact beyond all reasonable doubt that there is such a dimension as heaven where you would live in eternal bliss with God, then no one would really give a damn about the scientific arguments surrounding biblical miracles.

But there is no proof of any such afterlife worlds and all we can rely upon is our faith and our will to believe. The alternative however is unthinkable; eternal nothingness.

Deep down we are so uncertain with our inevitable death and what happens to us, that in many ways hatred for those with differing beliefs or differing race and cultural backgrounds is nothing more than an extension of our natural tendency to cling to life or fear death. There are no exceptions. The *death view* is the one single denominator that separates man's hatred with that of other living beings who are not capable of such emotions. It is the curse of the unenlightened.

The Skin Illusion and Radio Theory

Death is the great unanswered mystery of every person and birth's inevitable outcome. No phase of existence has the potential to unlock all of life's vital questions or give us the awareness of life's preciousness. There is no substitute for its knowledge and no factual knowledge that can be shared. No person including myself, cleric or scripture can prove anything about death. On the other hand, enlightenment holds as part of its characteristic the ability to relieve oneself of death's ignorance and thereby be relieved of its suffering. So while I am offering my own interpretation of what I understand to be the Buddhist view of death, I don't expect you to believe me. You would be a fool if you did. I'm not looking for anyone's approval. Some things however will touch greatly upon common sense and I believe worthy of word in spite of its extraordinary limited capacity.

As you sit reading this book in whatever space you might find yourself in, there are hundreds or perhaps millions of signals being broadcast through your space at this very moment. Television and radio signals from around the world, police conversations, military conversations, air traffic communications with airplanes, cell phone conversations, ham radio operators, truckers on CB radios, wireless internet signals, text messages, transmissions from outer space like those from satellites (and perhaps beyond), and a weather broadcast. They have no form or shape. You can't see them. You can't hear them. You can't feel them. You can't smell them. Yet they pass through you and your space harmlessly. You just need the right instrument to pick them up and give them form.

One misconception about Buddhism is that Buddhists believe in the theory of Reincarnation. In one sense that is true and in another it is not. The classic theory of the Hindu sort of Reincarnation involves a soul that moves from one existence to another. It suggests that while there may be an eternal soul, it is finite in space and has a form that can move from one space to another. So when a Buddhist talks about Reincarnating from one life to another, it is not at all the same. Buddhism deals with a concept known as *Transmigration*. In Transmigration, we talk about a consciousness and life force that has no form. It has eternally existed with an infinite past, an infinite future, and exists in infinite space.

Take that weather broadcast I just mentioned. If you possessed a weather radio it would have only one setting; either on or off. It can't be tuned to any other station other than the weather station. When you turn it on you start hearing the weather broadcast. So grab it for a moment and let's turn it on:

"…water temperature near the coast, 65 degrees. Coastal winds, 10 knots. Visibility, 3 miles with fog settling 10 miles from shore," then a pause. "This is the weather broadcast from the National Weather Service for Southern California and coastal areas of greater Los Angeles, including Orange County, and inland through Riverside County. Broadcasting on a frequency of 86.34 megahertz, 24 hours every day, this is the current weather and forecast as of 5:30 AM Pacific Time, Tuesday, June twenty fourth, two thousand and (whatever). Currently the air temperature inland is 66 degrees...," as it continues to the end and then starts all over again.

So now take a look at that radio as you hold it in your hand. It is creating a sound. Look around the room you're in. Do you see it anywhere else or is it only coming from the radio? Leaving the radio on, go ahead and place it on a table and walk into the another room. You can't see anything in here either, right? But you can still hear the weather report coming from the other room where you left the radio turned on. Now go back into the room and pick the radio up again. Turn it off and go back into that other room. Now turn the radio back on. Amazing! You are hearing it again in this other room coming from that same little radio. But it's no longer coming from the other room when you first turned it on. Turn it off again and take it outside. Turn it back on again. Amazing still! Almost everywhere you go you can still turn it off then on again and continue hearing the same broadcast.

While this may all sound quite silly it illustrates a very important point. While you may have taken the radio from one location to the other, you didn't actually take the signal with you because it has no form perceptible by our human senses. It's in the first room, in the second room, outside your house and perhaps miles and miles all around. That little radio contains nothing. You'll look at it while you are listening because that's where the sound is coming from. If you break it apart you won't find anything inside except circuitry and a battery for power. So let's do that shall we? Let's smash the radio and break it apart.

Did we destroy the broadcasted signal? Of course not. Is it still in the room and everywhere else we went to? Of course it is. The only difference is that we have no way of listening to it anymore. It has no form and was dependent upon that little radio to communicate with the "outside" world. It can no longer communicate no matter what we do. It is all around us but no longer has expression. It's gone but not gone. It exists, but it does not exist. Until we get another radio, the signal is still everywhere but in a state of dormancy.

Based upon my own understanding of Buddhism, I view life in a very similar common sense way. Our bodies are very much the same as the radio and our consciousness is very much the same as the radio signal. We may perceive that our lives are contained within our bodies as with the "soul" theory. The soul "exits" the body once it can no longer sustain life and moves on to another plane (wherever that might be). But I reject that concept completely. Instead we are nowhere and at the same time everywhere. Our lives are not contained within the surface of our skin any more than the broadcast was contained inside the plastic confines of the weather radio. But like the radio, the broadcast needs the device to express itself and our lives need our physical bodies to do the same.

When we die, the only thing that happens is that our bouncing karmic ball(s) freeze in their paths. When the right circumstances are created for another body to "pick up our signal", they begin moving again on their predetermined paths that were based on all the causes we've made in our past. And not just from the causes of the life that just ended but perhaps from lives even before.

Life can often be studied in its microcosmic form. Think of sleep. We all need it. Our bodies cannot function without the ability to rest and rejuvenate itself. Sleep can be quite pleasurable and often we even hate waking up in the morning because of how nice it feels. But if it feels so good, why wouldn't we want to stay asleep forever? It can be a suffering to wake up and likewise, so is birth. Would we even dare go to sleep if we thought we wouldn't wake up?   Think about it. Life's intent is the expression of itself. Otherwise, it's not life at all. Life's purpose is happiness. And there are no causes we can make while we are sleeping to help us achieve that. But we need to sleep none-the-less. So we go through a continuous cycle of sleeping and awakening throughout our entire lives. In terms of macrocosmic existence, this can be compared to an endless cycle of birth and death.

The entire physical world goes through continuous rhythms of birth and death.   From the smallest microscopic creature to the greatest galaxy in the universe, nothing in this dimension lasts. It is the way of the physical world. And so while I will suggest that our life "signals" and the karma it carries are eternal and last forever, the "radios" we use to make our causes and to express our lives (in the realm of the great incomprehensible vastness of time), are here for no more than a single moment of our eternal existence.

And so like the weather radio whose signal is more than one place at one time, so are we. You are right now sitting in this room. But you are also in that other room without leaving this room. You are out on your front lawn or in the street. You are in every city and every country. You are above the clouds, in all the oceans. You are on the moon, every planet in our solar system, and every other planetary system in the galaxy. Your life "signal" is as vast as the universe and therefore limitless. Yet the physical body you are using to express your life can only be in one place at one time just like the weather radio. But more importantly, it is an illusion that your life is limited within its immediate space. That is why you can have effects on people, places, and things that are even hundreds of miles away.

We are all part of an infinite ocean of life and when we die we don't really "go" anywhere. That's not to say that our consciousness doesn't experience a transition from life to death (*ke* to *ku*) as we also do from being awake to sleep. We simply remain everywhere in this state of *ku* until the conditions are right for another supreme organic high frequency receiver to pick up the signal from our life force and live again in the state of *ke*, allowing us to continue our karma from wherever we left off and occurs at the very moment of conception.

~~~

Some time in the late 90's I became very involved in interfaith organizations in Southern California and where I held board positions as a representative of Soka Gakkai International – USA (the name that would eventually replace NSA). Several of these groups sponsored an annual religious "trade show" of sorts called the Religious Diversity Fair held at the University of California/Irvine (UC Irvine). At one such event, I was asked to sit on a panel to represent the Buddhist view in a topic titled "Why Do Bad Things Happen to Good People?"

I sat at a table on a stage along with a Jewish Rabbi, a Catholic priest, Hindu priest, a Christian minister from one denomination, a Christian pastor from another denomination, a nun, and as I recall, the only other non-cleric member on the panel was a Muslim. I'll never forget one gentleman in the audience who was obviously struggling with a loss and beseeching the panel for an answer.

"My seventeen year old son died in a car crash just recently. It was only about six months ago. He was a good boy… a star member of the football team and an outstanding student." He continued as he began choking back tears. "I miss him so much and I'm having a very difficult time understanding all of this." He then sat back down and looked at us waiting for some answer that he hoped would relieve him of this pain.

I found it quite interesting that while the topic itself seemed quite direct, the conversation and inquiries from the audience kept moving more and more into the direction of "blame." And a lot of that was about blaming or not blaming God. In the case of this man, while it was clear we all felt his pain and sorrow, he was urged by several members on the panel not to find *blame* in God. Rather they tried to encourage him by instilling the idea that God works in mysterious ways and assured him that his son was with God. This was without exception everyone's basic answer.

Buddhism however, seemed the only philosophy at the table to actually offer a much different perspective. Finally the microphone was passed to me as I looked at him.

"Buddhism teaches that there is no such thing as a good person or bad person. There are only people who do good things or bad things," I said to him as I paused each moment wondering how to continue. "Or perhaps better put, we are all people capable of making causes that give value and enhancement to life or causes that slander and denigrate life through our thoughts, words, and actions. We are all capable of such things. Buddhism also teaches that life is eternal and that we cycle through birth and death throughout eternity the same way we sleep and wake up each night and each day.

Why for example is a child born in one house to a warm loving family and another born right next door to an abusive family? Why is a child born here in America and another born starving to death in some war torn area of Africa? Why are some children even born at all and some to a mother who chooses to abort before birth? Is it just random or is God playing a cruel game? If we claim to be 'blessed' by having been born in America or for the parents we have, then for what *reason* were we blessed? What did we do before birth that got us into that blessed status to begin with?

Death is a very painful experience and I am so sorry for your loss. You miss your son and will for the rest of your life. And while you are not a Buddhist, I sit here on a panel compelled to tell you my point of view and that's why we are here. And so I will speak frankly if that's OK without any expectation that you should believe what I am telling you."

The man nodded allowing me to continue. But then I began choking back even my own tears feeling the experience and loss of even my own daughter that I was not able to spend a single moment with let alone 17 years.

"We create our own karma or destinies... even the aborted child, the abused child, and the starving child. In Buddhism there are no innocents. We create causes in lifetime after lifetime meeting the consequences of those causes. Does that mean that Buddhism simply takes the position of '*so sorry too bad, but it was your fault to begin with anyway?*' Well in a sense yes, but ultimately Buddhism teaches that human beings are capable of changing their own karma if they are made aware of these capabilities and then taught how to use them. Without this knowledge we are unfortunately left with little choice other than to live through our karma. Having the karma of losing a son at 17 is your own and his death is his own. You and your son have always been together and will continue to meet each other in lifetime after lifetime as you already have in lifetime after lifetime even before this life. You miss him, but you will be together again... together again in *life*... not in death."

After I was done stating my position, I looked at the other members on the panel and couldn't help but feel their confusion and discomfort with what I said. I will leave it to your own speculation as to why that might be.

Seeking But Left in the Void

It's important to review this very crucial point. Mankind will forever be left in the dust behind scientific evolution if he cannot move himself past the self imposed limitations of blind acceptance. Religions built mainly upon literal prophecies and theoretical promises, will fall short of being able to handle the demands of our continued advancement. We cannot afford to ignore the *death view*.

There have been many self help gurus and methodologies that have sprung up over the last four decades including Warner Erhardt and E.S.T., Anthony Robbins, and most recently the ever growing popularity of *The Secret* just to name a few. All of these "schools" have merit and benefit and I have been a fan of a few of them myself. But they don't replace what religion is supposed to resolve and where it is perhaps failing in most cases.   They don't answer the questions that mankind *must* resolve; the ever standing mysteries of life and death.

The power of positive thinking is valid (important and even critical within Buddhism) and for the most part all of these methods are nothing more than different spins on many of the same messages that go all the way back to guys like Dale Carnegie and his book published in the 1930's, "<u>How to Win Friends and Influence People</u>." (Probably the best selling self help book of all time.)   But karma is still karma.   So for example, if you become a rich and powerful television star like Oprah Winfrey, it can be argued that it was not because she had changed any sort of karma but rather because she had already set into motion the causes that created the result no matter what she had to do to get there.   If you are having marital problems, weight problems, or financial problems and perhaps have resolved them through one thing or another be it through therapy, a financial self-help book, positive thinking, laws of attraction, visualization, or anything that helps you solve your issues then great!   But you are still expressing and acting out your karma... not changing it.

Let me create a simple analogy with having a car problem.   You take the car to your mechanic and he tells you that you should be using high octane gas instead of regular because of the high output turbo charged engine under the hood.   Well gee, you didn't know that.   So from that point on, you start spending the extra money on the higher grade gas and discover that your mechanic was absolutely correct.   Now your car is running like a champ. Does that mean you changed the destiny of your car or your own by simply putting better gas in the tank? Actually no, you didn't. Should it then have made any sense to use the better gas?   Don't be foolish! Of course it made sense!

Chapter 4

The Worlds in Which We Live

There is No Reality Except the One We Agree On

What do these words *Nam-myoho-renge-kyo* mean, and what caused over 10 million families in Japan to begin chanting these words to this scroll known as a *Gohonzon* (which I will explore in a later chapter) in an extraordinarily short period of time since the end of World War II? Well, maybe because they're Japanese after all and they're used to that sort of thing. Maybe it doesn't feel odd or foreign to them while for us, it's not an "American" thing to do. Frankly however, while there might be some cultural idiosyncrasies, in the end it's just perspective really.

What matters most is whether chanting these odd words have any merit. Chanting is easy don't you think? It seems odd especially for us westerners, but it's easy. It requires no thinking and best of all, no believing. Anyone can learn how to pronounce *Nam-myoho-renge-kyo* and say it over and over again. You don't need to have any special knowledge or go through some type of arduous training. *All I have to do is chant these words and all my dreams will come true?* Sounds like voodoo to me! And frankly, when I started chanting I couldn't have cared less if that's what it was. If it was going to help me solve my problems, what was there to lose except a bit of my own self infused dignity?

So the first thing one must understand is that chanting is experiential (even experimental at first) before theoretical. That's a good thing. In the first place, a "theory" always remains theory until it can be proven. Once proven it transfers from theory to fact or perhaps more appropriately put; a *proven* theory. The only unfortunate part here is that *fact* does not have to always be objective. In other words, think about the taste of one of your favorite foods like a big delicious juicy hamburger perhaps. To you the thought was a fact. But to me, it was theory since I wasn't the one who thought it and you can't prove it to me. Even with any of my own experiences in this book (some of which may seem quite trivial while some may seem amazing), the bottom line is and will always remain my own proven theory as a result of chanting. So while I'm going to blurt out an attempt to give you my take on why chanting works, it will forever remain a theory to those who do not chant.

The first thing that I would like to discuss is what I call the "mystical gap." That is, the gap between the awareness of our five senses that translates into thought and that which is beyond thought. If we both put on blind folds and someone holds up an onion to both our noses, we'll agree that it's an onion even though we've taken sight out of the picture. So based upon this relative association, while I don't know what an onion smells like to you because it's subjective, we've agreed it's an onion because what is relative to the smell of an onion to *you* smells like an onion to me based on my own relativity to *my* sense of what an onion smells like. But there is no way to prove that an onion smells the same to either one of us. Even if you scientifically understand the chemical compounds that create a smell and how our sense of smell reacts to it, it's just words on paper. We're going to *assume* for a moment that an onion smells the same to you as it does to me, but it's only because we've accepted that as a reality. Of course, we don't have to. We can actually say that no one really knows what an onion smells like. We have to create the assumption that the smell of an onion is the same to everyone in order to function in the world we call "reality."

So what I've done here is taken a simple example and caused it to enter the mystical gap. Looked at in these terms, there is nothing that can be proven. The only reality is *your* reality. Objective reality only exists because we agreed upon it. But no one can prove it exists. Let's take a more difficult example. A soldier is killed in a war. We both read it in the newspaper and his body is returned for burial. There is a family in bereavement and we can prove beyond doubt that the soldier is no longer alive. Our realities seem to match and this appears to prove there is an objective reality. We can even read the newspaper article out loud together word for word and prove even further that what you read is the same as what I read. But no matter what, we accept and therefore create objective reality. We've agreed upon something. We've agreed that we read the same thing. We've agreed that the soldier was killed in a battle. It can be proven! But (and here is the big BUT), it is proven based upon the *theory* that our experience was the same. In the end however, it's still two subjective realities agreeing to create one that *becomes* objective because we made it so. This is part of a concept called *dependent origination* which I will also discuss a bit later. But for a moment let me present you with this:

Let's say that when you are born an alien spaceship takes you to an Earth-like planet where you are the only inhabitant besides vegetation. The aliens make sure that through whatever technology is necessary, you are fed, clothed, and have shelter. Obviously you would never learn to speak. You would learn to make sounds like grunts from pain when you stubbed your toe. You would learn that there is a difference between a blue sky and a grey sky, but you would never know a color is a color because you have no other person to agree with you on the matter. Theoretically, you may at some point become a vegetable yourself as your mind would have no stimulation and like a muscle never used, go into atrophy. Reality therefore is totally based and reliant upon other living beings.   Most importantly for us humans it's having other humans. We rely upon each other to create our reality.

So is the rock itself hard or is it hard because we agree it's hard? Oh what a mystery! Philosophers and scientists for centuries have been arguing and discussing what constitutes this dimension we call "reality." Frankly, it doesn't matter to me. All that matters is that there is a mystery that gaps our sensory perceptions and any ultimate truth.   This is what can be termed as *"mystical."*

So while trying to display that even our reality is a mystery which is incomprehensible, take the more obvious mysteries like existence, essence, eternity, life, death, and the universe itself. We would agree that our minds cannot perceive infinity. I remember sitting in grade school thinking about dividing an inch into a half an inch, into a quarter inch, into an eighth, into a sixteenth and on and on... it could never end.   I concluded that nothingness was impossible as well as unperceivable. There is much we don't understand and much we can never understand even if we tried. Our brains have a limited capacity in understanding and perhaps agree that what we can't understand we can call *"mystical"*; perhaps for lack of a better word.

If I were to say the words greed, anger, despair, joy, disappointment, infatuation, etc., you know what I'm talking about because you've experienced all of these emotions. Your brain has created a point of reference for all these things but one thing you can't answer is this: *where did these emotions come from?*

While we may have institutions that teach anger *management*, we never had (nor ever needed) any courses that taught us how to *become* angry. We possessed it from birth. The very first day something was taken away from us and boom, here come the tears! The idea that we are born as blank slates is ludicrous and totally illogical. Buddhism suggests we inherently exist in what are called "worlds." A world is a place that happens to dominate your reality at any given moment and Buddhism teaches that there are ten of them:

1. Hell

     The world of complete despair and hopelessness.

2. Hunger

     The world of "want" and desire where greed lives.

3. Anger

     The world of ego where one feels they are right while others are wrong.

4. Animality

     The world where one takes advantage of those who may be weaker or when cowering to those who appear stronger.

5. Tranquility

     The world where we are pretty much "at ease" with where we are at.

6. Heaven or Rapture

     The world characterized by elation, jubilation, euphoria, excitement, and exhilaration.

7. Learning

The world where we are engaged in gathering knowledge or understanding of something.

8. Absorption

The world where what we have learned or understand becomes useful and one with the moment.

9. Mercy or Bodhisattva

The world where we take on the suffering of another as that of our own and become consumed with relieving that suffering. Essentially it's when we care about the happiness of others.

10. Wisdom, Buddhahood, or Enlightenment

It's certainly easy to talk about 1 through 9 as we can all relate from experience. Number 10 is the tough one but let's not worry about that right now. Let's review for a moment these worlds based on what we've just discussed. They are based on an agreed upon reality but they are mystical since we have no idea where they came from as none of these things can be "learned" any more than you can teach a blind person the difference between blue and grey. If we discuss anger for example, we are only capable of having this discussion based on a reference we have both experienced. Once again, two separate realities that equal the same reference point like the onion. Actually without BOTH of us having had the experience, one could not explain what anger was to the other. If I never smelled an onion, could you explain it to me so that I would know what you are talking about? Of course not!

You don't have to be considered a "mystic" to agree that it is impossible for our conscious, calculating, analytical brains to understand everything. Again, we are referring to this as mystical.

In the process of humankind's spiritual evolution, we have entered into a time where worded "explanations" of everything are no longer necessary. This is now a time when our scientific evolution can live in harmony with our spiritual evolution. In a short time we will come to the conclusion that one cannot live without the other or perhaps better put, one without the other will continue to lead to continued pain and destruction. Mankind required much of his religiosity to maintain sanity. At one time we believed Apollo, the Greek God of the Sun, dragged the sun across the sky. Columbus was warned not to venture to the "New World" for fear that his ships would fall off the edge of the planet. In fact science has wound down just about everything that once required religious explanation to where the only thing left is that which science cannot explain or even hope to ever explain: life itself. And I don't mean it in the terms of origin like the continued debate surrounding the physical evolution of our species. In the use of the word, I refer to the matter of life, death, and the infinite and within life the origin of such things as the Ten Worlds.

So while the origin of anger is mystical, the existence of it is inarguable. You possess the potential at this very moment to be angry. But what would it

take?   There would need to be an of external event
(which includes the memory of one) for you to stimulate
a state that currently is dormant and in this case, the
World of Anger.

I prefer how Buddhism refers to these states as
"worlds" as opposed to emotions because the word
emotion really encompasses the totality of the place you
are in.   An emotion is certainly defined as an affective
state of consciousness, but a "world" is a sphere of
existence.

~~~

Tom sits on a couch in his 25th floor apartment
intensely watching a professional basketball game
between the New York Knicks and the Boston Celtics.
He had received inside information from his bookie that
Eddy Curry, New York's best player, was coming into
the game with a stomach virus.   With Stephon Marbury
out for two more games with an injury, Boston was the
sure underdog bet.

There were only 7 seconds left on the clock and
in spite of New York's undermanned talent, the bench
had risen to the occasion.   New York has the ball after
getting thrown out of bounds by Boston.   The Celtics
call a time out and a commercial comes on.

If Boston's defense can hold off New York for 7
seconds, just 7 seconds, Boston wins and life becomes
good again for Tom.   In spite of his gambling addiction,
Tom thought this was the last of it.   One more bet; one
more bet to make it right.   But even if Curry were really
sick, he certainly didn't show it as Boston was in the
lead by only one measly point, 97 to 96.   The Celtics

needed to win. Boston needs to hold off New York for 7 seconds without allowing them to score! He felt as though his life was hanging in the balance of a 7 second clock.

His wife Claire had already been threatening to leave him and had suggested a divorce. Tom loved more than anything his wife and children. The thought of losing them was devastating. He was so certain in winning this "last bet" he took every last nickel he could muster up to place on it. Unbeknownst to Claire, he cashed out over $50,000 in his 401K. It was all they had left after losing his job three months earlier. Times had become hard. Creditors were calling on a daily basis and with Claire being the only one working; they could barely make the rent and keep themselves from being evicted. But a win would net him over $200,000 and surely save his marriage and family. He wouldn't even have to tell Claire how he got it. Just put the money back into the 401K and bank the rest in a secret account taking out what they would need as he continues looking for another job.

THE WORLD OF HEAVEN OR RAPTURE

The commercial is over. They're back. The announcer begins talking, "New York has the ball only 7 seconds left on the clock. Boston up by one point."

A New York Knick standing out of bounds holds the ball over his head looking for an open man as the Celtics scramble trying to cover the remaining four Knicks on the court.

The announcer continues, "What the Knicks need to try and do is get the ball to Curry as it seems he's really come alive this fourth quarter... drive to the basket and even hope to draw a penalty. With Curry at the free throw, it's hard to imagine he wouldn't make at least one and tie this game up."

"Frye with the ball looking for the open man.... he finds Jefferson... Jefferson covered well by Gomes. Spinning around Gomes, the pass intended for Curry." The announcer screams, "Batted away by Pierce what a defensive play! The ball rolls down the court as time has run out and the Celtics win 97 to 96!"

Tom leaps from the couch screaming at the top of his lungs. Jumping up and down like a kid on a trampoline shouting, "We won! We won!" Bouncing on the couch he accidentally hits the television remote control and accidentally switches to a PBS channel. The Italian Puccini opera "Gianni Schicchi" is being performed. On the screen a young woman sings to an older man.

In his excitement Tom wrestles to find the channel changer on the control, but stops for a moment and stares at the opera singer.

The part of this story is where the young daughter (Lauretta) forbidden by her father (Gianni Schicchi) to marry her love Rinuccio, pleads with him that he would only leave her the alternative of killing herself by jumping off Ponte Vecchio (the old bridge of Florence).

O mio babbino caro,	*My dear father,*
mi piace è bello, bello;	*I love him, he's beautiful, beautiful;*
vo'andare in Porta Rossa	*I want to go to Porta Rossa*
a comperar l'anello!	*and buy the ring!*
Sì, sì, ci voglio andare!	*Yes, yes, I want to go!*
e se l'amassi indarno,	*And if my love is in vain,*
andrei sul Ponte Vecchio,	*I would go upon Ponte Vecchio*
ma per buttarmi in Arno!	*only to jump in the Arno (the river in Florence)*
Mi struggo e mi tormento!	*I long for him and torment myself*
O Dio, vorrei morir!	*O God, I'd like to die!*
Babbo, pietà, pietà!	*Father, have pity, have pity!*

While Tom knows nothing about opera, nothing about the story and can't understand a word being sung, it's the most beautiful sound he believes he has ever heard. He watches her sing as tears begin to come down her face. Tom begins to cry with her as he is overwhelmed by joy. *"Why,"* he thought, *"had I never known how beautiful opera is?"*

As he turns up the volume, he wishes he could grab and hold her; sing with her, be one with her.

Standing up again from the couch he stretches out his arms looking up at the ceiling but he sees no ceiling. The bright whiteness is the unlimited sky itself.

Dropping his arms and looking back at the opera singer Tom wipes the tears from his eyes. Pivoting around he looks over at the sliding glass door leading to the balcony. Moving towards it, he pulls the door open along its track. The wind of a cool spring air touches the moistness of his tears as young Lauretta continues her plea.

Stepping out onto the balcony everything seemed so perfect. Grabbing a hold of the railing, Tom looks straight ahead and out at the city with its lights against the dimming dusk sky. He fills his lungs with the magnificent air. He feels blessed. Nothing could be more perfect than this moment, this city, this music, and this balcony.

THE WORLD OF HELL

The commercial is over. They're back. The announcer begins talking, "New York has the ball only 7 seconds left on the clock. Boston up by one point."

A New York Knick out of bounds holds the ball over his head looking for an open man as the Celtics scramble trying to cover the remaining four Knicks on the court.

The announcer continues, "What the Knicks need to try and do is get the ball to Curry as it seems he's really come alive this fourth quarter… drive to the basket and even hope to draw a penalty. With Curry at the free throw, it's hard to imagine he wouldn't make at least one and tie this game up."

"Frye with the ball looking for the open man…. he finds Jefferson… Jefferson covered well by Gomes. Spinning around Gomes, a beautiful pass to Curry… Pierce tries to bat it away but just misses!" The announcer screams, "Not enough time on the clock to drive in, Curry fades back and shoots. There's the buzzer! Curry makes the basket! The Knicks take the win 98 to 97! What a pass by Gomes and what a shot by Curry!"

Tom leaps from the couch screaming at the top of his lungs. "No No! NO! My God no!" Grabbing the first thing he can find, he throws the television remote control across the room hitting a lamp. While grabbing it, he accidentally switches the television to a PBS channel. The Italian Puccini opera "Gianni Schicchi" is being performed. On the screen a young woman is singing to an older man.

Tom numbly falls back down on the couch. He stares at the opera singer as her tears fall, pleading to the man before her.

O mio babbino caro,	*My dear father,*
mi piace è bello, bello;	*I love him, he's beautiful, beautiful;*
vo'andare in Porta Rossa	*I want to go to Porta Rossa*
a comperar l'anello!	*and buy the ring!*
Sì, sì, ci voglio andare!	*Yes, yes, I want to go!*

e se l'amassi indarno,	*And if my love is in vain,*
andrei sul Ponte Vecchio,	*I would go upon Ponte Vecchio*
ma per buttarmi in Arno!	*only to jump in the Arno (the river in Florence)*
Mi struggo e mi tormento!	*I long for him and torment myself*
O Dio, vorrei morir!	*O God, I'd like to die!*
Babbo, pietà, pietà!	*Father, have pity, have pity!*

While Tom knows nothing about opera, nothing about the story and can't understand a word being sung, it fills his heart with pain. He has lost everything. His wife and his children will be gone once they have discovered what he has done. Every note of her song feels like a tightening squeeze around his throat.

Tom begins to hyper-ventilate as he stands up. He needs air. Turning around, he moves to the sliding glass door leading to the balcony and pulls it open. The cold evening spring air slaps his face as he tries to take it in but he can only gasp as he moves to the balcony railing.

The singing of young Lauretta makes the tragic life of Tom all the more real as he can only look down at the street 25 stories below. He thinks of his wife Claire and his two young girls and blames himself for all the pain they have suffered because of him. Nothing will change and nothing will be better. While they will also suffer the pain of his death, it will be short lived and far better than any further anguish he could cause them to suffer. The $50,000 he lost in their retirement savings will be 10 times greater from his life insurance policy. Claire is young and beautiful. She will find someone worthy of her.

As Tom begins to cry from the pain he feels from already missing them he steps over the railing. Balancing himself on the small ledge and leaning his weight back against the railing, Tom spreads his arms out and looks up at the sky. It is dark. It is the last thing he will see and Lauretta's threat to her father Gianni Schicchi to jump from a bridge, the last thing he will hear.

~~~

Two distinguishing worlds: Heaven and Hell. Putting aside for a moment the idea of emotion, look through Tom's eyes. It is not just that he is either overwhelmed by joy or overcome by the deepest possible despair; his entire environment and everything around him has become part of a *world*. As Tom sat there on his couch awaiting the outcome of the game, he had not yet entered either the Worlds of Heaven or Hell while both potentials were latent. One was going to happen. When in Heaven, everything was a part of it; the music for which he had never appreciated, the bright whiteness of the ceiling was boundless, all the way to the balcony from which he could bask in his ecstasy. When taken into the World of Hell, the room closed in on him where he could not breathe and finally, the balcony became an instrument where he committed the ultimate act of a person in the World of Hell. Even though he could not understand Italian and the words of Lauretta's song, they became part of one world or the other.

And to think, the difference between one of these worlds or the other was a simple action that happened in just a moment. More importantly while latent, these worlds were triggered by external experiences as is true with all Ten Worlds. They don't just come about on their own. The theory of the Buddhist Ten Worlds is very fascinating and I encourage you to find further study on them. Actually Buddhism states that there are 3000 possibilities in a single moment of life known as *ichinen sanzen*. It claims that each of the Ten Worlds contains within them the Ten Worlds, within what are known as the ten factors and three realms of existence; hence $10 \times 10 \times 10 \times 3 = 3000$.

Let's not move too far away from the mystical reality of Tom's worlds. Once again, they are not mystical from the point of view that we get the story, understand the differences, and can see the logic in it. But again I beg to ask, where did they come from? Did Tom "learn" them or were they always there? For me, it is personally illogical to consider those worlds having been learned. How would you teach a little baby despair when denied the milk of its mother? Therefore, there must be a of "trigger" that knocks you from one world into another.

So as mentioned before, reason can only conclude that these worlds existed since birth and will until death. Human life, in fact all life is endowed with the existence of the Ten Worlds. We can be in any one of these worlds at any moment while the other nine remain in a latent state waiting for the right conditions.

People are also dominated by one world or another.   Our tendency is to gravitate towards a particular world. Personally, I would tend to say that the world that I've always gravitated towards is the World of Tranquility (number five). I like referring to it as the World of the Couch Potato where everything is pretty much even keeled.   Relaxation... no stress... ahhhhhhhhhhhhhhh! That's where laziness also lives. If you look at Tom, perhaps his dominant world is the World of Rapture addicted to the "high" one gets from winning. It's been said however that the back door to the World of Heaven is the World of Hell.   That was made quite evident in the story.

If you think about it, any of these dominating worlds can in the end be destructive and lead to a life less lived. The objective then is to make an attempt to shift our dominating world to one that helps us create more value with our lives and ultimately leads to happiness and fulfillment. And when I say "fulfillment" I certainly don't mean a fleeting moment of fulfillment.

This now brings us to the elusive and perhaps abstract tenth world: the World of Buddhahood or Enlightenment. If you look at the first nine worlds, it's not hard to see that they all exist and based upon our mutual experiences we can agree that they exist as an objective fact. It is however with your indulgence that I must now move towards theory in order to explain this tenth world and how one gets there. I'm hoping that at the very least we can agree on the following:

1. We can relate and agree that we all possess the first nine worlds.
2. It is "mystical" as to why we have them or where they come from.
3. Each world requires a "trigger" or external stimulus to bring them about.

First I will characterize the World of Enlightenment as best I can or at least what comes to my mind:

1. Birth and death: The ability to lift the veil of our ignorance since it is the ignorance of birth and death that causes us to suffer from it.
2. Wisdom: The ability to "see" your destiny and work to avoid or lessen the consequences of negative causes made in the past. Bear in mind, it's not that your brain can actually perceive the bouncing ball and where it came from or where it is about to hit. But that wouldn't be "wisdom" to begin with. It takes place in a far deeper level of consciousness. It is the only means by which karma can actually be changed.
3. Liberation from illusion: There are quite a few of them that I could mention, but I think the most important of which is our ability to move away from that which we *think* will make us happy to what we actually *need* to be happy. This does

not mean we stop pursuing whatever goals we may have, but in the process of doing so we begin understanding the difference between wants and needs particularly in terms of happiness. This also involves shedding our illusion of permanence. Nothing in our material outer world lasts forever and is in constant change. In so doing, we can lessen our attachments to the outer world while at the same time use it to accomplish our inner and unattached happiness.

4. Human Revolution: In the process of shifting our dominant world to that of the tenth world, we need to go through a process of change. We cannot continue making causes that work against us. But as the saying goes, *we* are our own worst enemy. So a transformation of our "negative" tendencies becomes vitally necessary and it's not so much that we begin some sort of psychological analysis of why we are this way or that. (This is not to diminish the need for psychology and its place as part of modern medicine.) But as part of the character of our wisdom, we will use (and perhaps at times even place ourselves within) negative circumstances to learn and extract from our lives the inclinations that do harm to ourselves and others even if we are not consciously aware of them. More importantly as the term suggests our "humanity" begins to revolt against our lesser

selves so that we can emerge as true human beings worthy of the title.

All forms of Buddhism at their core value have as their ultimate objective the ability to attain or realize this World of Enlightenment. There is often an error among westerners who interpret "Buddha" as the Buddhist version of God. Rather, a Buddha is anyone who achieves (or is within) this tenth world. So actually anyone has the potential to be a Buddha. Where many religions have as their purpose some fanciful world to be attained after death, Buddhism's purpose is one of *life* experience not death experience.

This then brings us to the chanting of *Nam-myoho-renge-kyo*. Theory once again, just theory but please hang in with me.

In the quest for enlightenment, many Buddhist sects necessitate incredibly arduous practices. Luckily for you I'm not an expert of all the many different sects of Buddhism or I might be tempted to bore you with detailed comparisons between one sect and another. Instead, I would prefer to just focus on the simplistic and once again theoretically profound practice of chanting these words.

~~~

The discovery of this practice happened a little over 700 years ago in 13th century Japan when a Buddhist priest known as Nichiren begged a logical question which can certainly be applied to our world today: Why with all these religions, is there still so much agony and a world filled with people still lost for answers regarding how to relieve their suffering in life caused by such things as hatred, war, disease, and financial strife? *"The rationale for religions after all,"* he thought *"was for that very purpose."*

Promising at the age of 12 to seek an answer, he entered a Buddhist temple to begin his education and where four years later he decided to remain at the temple and be ordained a priest. He quickly gained a reputation for his insatiable and intense study of all forms of Buddhism each of which derived from the teachings of the first Buddha known as Shakyamuni or Gautama Buddha who lived in India around 500 BC. He's the famous guy from which all those statues were erected across Asia from India through China, Southeast Asia like Vietnam and Cambodia and finally into Japan. His teachings were compiled in what are known as "sutras." While the number of these teachings is really not important what matters is the multitude of Buddhist sects derived from all these various sutras and resulting interpretations of what constitutes what Buddhism is *suppose* to be. I would say similarly to what happened with other religions around the world. In fact you may very easily find this true with all religions.

What was the clear intent of Jesus? What was the clear intent of Mohammed? What was the clear intent of Shakyamuni Buddha? All fair and logical questions considering the consequential hatred, war, and senseless killings that resulted from these splintered interpretations throughout the centuries into our present time. And even though Buddhism may not share the same sort of violent history as is common fact with

Islam, Hinduism, Judaism, and Christianity, it none-the-less was doing very little to alleviate the human suffering that was as widespread in 13th century Japan as it is throughout the world today.

Based on an expansive view, have the religions of the world failed their founder's purpose of relieving the suffering of their adherents? Instead, do they only offer an attempt to bring meaning, comfort, and solutions to suffering by instilling blind faith hope of a better world that is not *of* this world or *of* this lifetime? This was what was so puzzling to Nichiren and why he unrelentingly began a quest to discover the core truth of Buddhism if in fact one even existed. What was Shakyamuni's intent? It was then, after 14 years of dedicated study of all the Buddhist doctrines when he determined that the conclusion of Shakyamuni's teachings was contained in the sutra known as the *Lotus Sutra*.

The mystery contained in this sutra was that Shakyamuni kept mentioning something about a "law" and while describing it as the "one" law which could lead all living beings to that tenth world, did not clearly say what it was. Instead, he predicted that a character described as *Bodhisattva Jogyo* would eventually reveal this law and propagate it to the world when the time was correct.

Nichiren discovered that this "law" was actually contained within the title of the sutra itself (Myoho Renge Kyo) and that by devoting one's life to it (Nam) one would be able to attain Enlightenment within a single lifetime. It was on April 28, 1253 that Nichiren chanted these words for the very first time and realized this as Shakyamuni's final conclusive intent and method for common modern everyday folks like you and I to achieve this state. Shakyamuni alluded to this "law" but never specifically revealed what it was.

It's hard to avoid religious dogma since nothing I am about to tell you can be proven through the written word. But again, I can only prove that a place like the third world, the World of Anger for example, exists only because you *know* it does based on your experience and our agreed up relativity to that experience. So as to the World of Buddhahood, there really is no difference except that most of us don't know we even have this world as a potential. Without *experiencing* it you cannot know it as your own relative fact just as with the other nine worlds.

This is then another area where Buddhism differs from most other religions in that it is based upon practice before belief. I can call myself a "non-practicing" Jew, Christian, or Muslim while never attending any temples, churches or mosques. It would be quite socially acceptable to say so. Nor do I need to follow the prescribed precepts of prayer, yet still can "tag" myself as such based upon my belief or upbringing. This is because belief supersedes practice. We often hear expressions such as "accepting" Jesus as your savior as the first step in becoming a Christian. The same can be said of Islam. And while Jews show very little interest in proselytizing Judaism, it is none-the-less a belief system first and foremost.

It would be an oxymoron however for a Buddhist to profess to be a Buddhist without actually *practicing* Buddhism. Well I suppose you *could*, but it would not make any sense. It would be like saying I'm an archer without ever lifting a bow and arrow. This is not to say that belief does not play some part in Buddhism, but as the expression is often heard in Buddhism, "faith equals action" which essentially means you cannot separate one from the other. A Buddhist is not a Buddhist if he or she does not actually practice. This is a very important point and you'll see where I am going with this.

Shakyamuni discussed the essence of his teachings as contained in a "law." Nichiren identified that law as being within the title of the Lotus Sutra, *Myoho Renge Kyo*. Borrowing from the dictionary for a moment, by "law" he means: A statement describing a relationship observed to be invariable between or among phenomena for all cases in which the specified conditions are met: as in *the law of gravity*.

All religions have their own "laws," but this is quite different because like gravity it cannot be grasped through belief but rather only through the experience of its actual existence. There would be no point in playing golf if you were not mindful that the law of gravity existed. Likewise, there is no point in practicing Buddhism if there is no proof of its affects.

So like it or not, here I go spewing out what will seem to be religious dogma as I'm about to explain the principle of chanting *Nam Myo Renge Kyo* to this scroll called the *Gohonzon*. As I'm doing so, you must please bear in mind what I've said over and over again which at this point is redundant add nauseum; I can't prove it in a book anymore than I can prove by simply telling you that if you jump off a diving board you'll hit the water. A scientist might object, *"NO! It can be proven that all objects in the universe attract one another. If object A has mass* Ma *and object B has mass* Mb, *then the force (F) on object A is directed toward object B and has magnitude!"* It's still a theory for goodness sake! A PROVEN theory that we now agree to accept as fact, but a theory none-the-less! You are only creating theorem to that which we know exists. So likewise, here is how we prove that the World of Enlightenment or Buddhahood exists:

The literal loosely translated meaning of *Nam-myoho-renge-kyo* is somewhat irrelevant, but you would probably be angry with me if I didn't at least mention it and perhaps think I was hiding something. OK, I'll say it once and then leave it alone: *"Devotion to the mystic law of cause and effect through sound or the Buddha's teachings."* Satisfied? It didn't prove anything however did it? I'm sorry. But what matters is this: All worlds require conditions with which to elicit a response. Tom's worlds were elicited by hearing the announcer say in version number one, "The ball rolls down the court as time has run out and the Celtics win 97 to 96!" Those words immediately threw him into the sixth world, the World of Heaven. In version number two the announcers words "There's the buzzer! Curry makes the basket! The Knicks take the win 98 to 97!" These words activated his lowest world, the World of Hell. So we know that words, sounds, visuals, events, etc. mystically bring about all of these mystic worlds that are latent within our lives. As such, the words *Nam-myoho-renge-kyo* are the words that our tenth world hears which is obviously created by our own voice even if by thought alone. Tom experienced a "law" so to speak; the law of action and reaction, of cause and effect. We can talk all day long about how Tom put himself in that position to begin with (theory), but his reaction was based on law. There is a mystic communication that occurs between the Ten Worlds and our outer world. They are all the same in that regard.

So in conclusion, you have the theory that object A has mass *Ma* and object B has mass *Mb*, then the force (*F)* on object A is directed toward object B and has magnitude = the law of gravity. Well OK then, by causing disturbances from particle to particle along a medium through patterns of vibrations expressed in the equation of sound created by *Df* (*Nam* + *Myoho* + *Renge* + *Kyo*) as directed toward object *G* (Gohonzon) = the World of Buddhahood. And there you have it. Are these two theories valid? Well to a person born and raised floating in outer space, gravity wouldn't mean a damn thing until he got to some larger *Ma* (mass) such as a planet and experienced this law.

Chapter 5

The World's Oldest Profession

Prior to 1980, much happened after my return to New York and first began my Buddhist practice. At around the same time I arrived in 1976, a strong contingent of NSA members (particularly in New York City) began rejecting the overbearing and somewhat cultish direction that the national leadership of George Williams and NSA was moving in. As a result, the organization entered into what was called "Phase II." The idea was to become a "softer" organization focusing more on study, dialogue, and less on trying to recruit new members.

While the organization grew somewhat stagnant, we were all extremely excited when it was announced that New York would get its own Nichiren Shoshu priest imported directly from the head temple in Japan *and* our very own Buddhist temple. A Buddhist priest! This was big news. Up to that time the only temples and priests were in Washington DC, Chicago, California, and Hawaii. The bestowing of *Gohonzons* was always conducted by a priest. In New York we had to wait until the priest stationed in Washington DC came up to conduct the ceremony. *But a priest in New York?* A new era was about to begin. After all, what better authority on Buddhism than a Buddhist priest and a temple to boot!

And so it came to pass that in the late 1970's New York welcomed Reverend Tono from Japan and the opening of our new Nichiren Shoshu Temple in Flushing, Queens, New York. Now New York members could get the "pure" message of Buddhism from a man in robe dedicated to nothing other than the practice of this Buddhism and study of its principles. Little did we know however that this priest would end up tearing apart the lay membership and nearly destroying the entire New York City organization.

Apparently there was a dispute of some kind going on within the hierarchy of the head temple in Japan regarding who the "true" high priest was. I didn't know the details at the time (and won't bore you with them anyway), but suffice it to say a group of priests known as "Sho-Shinkai" felt that another priest should have rightly inherited the throne and started an anti-Nikken Abe campaign (Nikken Abe being the newly appointed high priest of the head temple near Mount Fuji in Japan). In addition, this group of priests also began spewing anti-Soka Gakkai/NSA rhetoric probably because our organization (reluctantly, passively, or otherwise) was willing to recognized Nikken Abe as the high priest. Tono (as it just so happened) turned out to be Sho-Shinkai. A power struggle within the clergy had ensued and while we really didn't know what was going on, we the members got caught in the middle.

As Tono continued to denunciate the lay organization of Soka Gakkai and its American branch of NSA, we were of course compelled to listen. Members started getting discouraged and one at a time began leaving. Some stuck with Tono and others with NSA, but most just faded away. For myself, I was so confused that I just didn't want to have anything to do with anyone. For one thing, we were not getting any clear information about what was going on and secondly I was simply discouraged with the whole organized religion thing. Although not about to stop practicing Buddhism, I had little interest in continuing with either side. It was not a very easy time for me personally as I was in a troubled marriage, just graduating from college, and starting a new career.

Without the contact of any other Buddhists and a shift in priorities, chanting each day was slowly but surely tapering off until I stopped chanting altogether. In fact, I eventually saw little point in keeping my *Gohonzon* enshrined and put it away.

The loss of the baby only made things worse as Marcia became ever more depressed, wouldn't go back to work, and took up smoking again. After about a year and a half as an assistant producer, I concluded that advertising was just not the place for me. So in the spring of 1980, I looked at going back into broadcasting and put in an application as a summer vacation engineer with NBC just as I had done with ABC.

I got the gig and while things went quite well at my new job, I was growing more and more distraught with home life. It turned into a depressing and incredibly stressful marriage that was remaining in force for over four years because of the pregnancy. Rather than deal with the continued torment we had to finally end it. We even tried marriage therapy but it came to a point when even the therapist seemed to conclude that this was no longer a union to be saved but instead began helping us dissolve a no-win situation.

I found another apartment in Queens but it seemed Marcia was less ready for the change than me. The following months would be brutal. In spite of the fact that we had little or no possessions except a cat to quibble over (including no children), Marcia was just not prepared to let go. I believe to this day that while we made the choice not to have an abortion, our baby had the wisdom to know what was best for itself and for her parents. I was ready to move on with my life and apparently Marcia was not. And so at this point while there was no way to rectify the situation between the two of us, the only thing left for her to do was make the separation as uncomfortable for me as possible.

The state of New York required a one year period of "legal" separation followed by a divorce that would make the separation agreement the binding divorce decree. However after the year had passed, she began refusing to sign the final document. The stress became nearly unbearable for me. While of course I had no one to blame except myself, I was being held in a marriage that should have never taken place to begin with. I can't say I didn't have it coming to me but couldn't fathom what her intention was other than vindictiveness from perhaps a perception that she was abandoned.   I was most definitely held within the furious hell of a woman scorned. I had already stopped practicing Buddhism and for whatever reason hadn't even considered it as a solution to the situation. So instead I struggled with various health problems mainly caused by persistent insomnia, stress, and paranoia. Although I managed not to let it affect my job, at times I felt like I was losing my mind.

I wasn't the pocket protector guy in public school, but I wasn't very involved with sports either. And if you weren't involved in sports in those days, you were pretty much a "nobody." The most popular girls were only interested in the "jocks." I was tall, thin, and good looking but it made little difference.   Things changed a bit in 11th grade but it was hard to shed all that broken self-esteem from a dozen or so childhood years of reclusion, exclusion, and occasional bullying. The pain of those years never leaves as so many can understand.

So once the separation took place, I immediately embarked on a personal vanity make-over mission. I joined a health club, dropped over 30 pounds (after gaining some 50 pounds since graduating high school), and started dating. Through the urging of friends and colleagues, I was even picked up by a major modeling agency though I never really became serious about the profession.   I did however land a couple of TV commercials and a quick one time bit part on the TV soap *One Life to Live*.   So while I was really into my looks, it became a daily burden when I began attempting to use it as a means to make money.

My NBC gig was the quintessential schedule for a single guy living in New York City.   I began working on a new project called Talknet which was NBC Radio's nationally syndicated talk show.   The show I was assigned to was a financial advice program hosted by a Bruce Williams who was followed by Sally Jesse Raphael before her TV stardom and daytime talk show took off.   My show ran Monday through Friday from 7:00 PM until 10:00 PM.   So technically I didn't have to be in until about 4:00 PM but most times not even until 6:00 PM and was able to leave right after the show.   I had plenty of time to work out at the health club mid-morning, enjoy my day, get to work, and get myself back into Manhattan to go "clubbing" at some of New York's hottest dance clubs and singles bars such as Heartbreak and the China Club.   Of course nothing really got moving at the clubs until around 11:00 PM anyway.   So it was just perfect to party late, sleep in, exercise, work, and then party some more!

So while I was certainly making the most of the New York single life I was also stuck with this unsigned divorce decree that I desperately wanted to get behind me.   Finally, it came to a point where I had no other choice but to threaten Marcia financially with a lawsuit since it was already unreasonable to continue her refusal to sign the documents.   It was only then that she finally agreed to make a trip to the attorney's office and ended it.

While it seemed like it was everything I wanted, I developed a mental addiction to going out at night. In fact it almost became impossible to stay home after work and do something like read a book or watch television. The routine was always the same. Hop on the subway after the show, get back to my apartment in Jackson Heights, change my clothes, hop on my Honda V65 Saber motorcycle or return to the subway and head back into Manhattan. I would usually get to one of my favorite clubs by around 11:30 PM and party until the crowd thinned out which was usually about 2:00 to 3:00 in the morning (later on Friday and Saturdays). On weekdays, I would get back to my apartment and in bed by 3:00 AM, sleep until about 10:00 AM, meet my best friend Jimmy (who worked Sally Jesse Raphael's show) to pump iron, get back to my apartment at about 1:00 PM, shower, get dressed and head back to the NBC studios for work. What a life! Or so it seemed.

I had quite a few relationships with women some long term and some very short. These were the "me generation" Reagan 80's and I was playing it to the hilt. While not averse to getting into a monogamous commitment with the right woman, I was also not hesitant to quickly cut anything off that didn't feel right. After what I had gone through with Marcia even a woman who smoked cigarettes was instantaneously deemed a disqualified candidate. In many ways (not as bad as some in those days and certainly not as bad as others) I was a pretty loose cannon. (No pun intended of course.) Though I couldn't see it in myself, I know that I had become self absorbed and arrogant. But I was a very sensitive bastard (for those who saw me as one) and think I always remained good hearted and never intentionally looked to hurt or use anyone. It's just how it came out and who I was at the time. Frankly, I was an addict pure and simple.   Addicted to the nightlife, addicted to women, and like that 80's song went: *"addicted to love."*

It was Saturday, December 31st, 1983 and New Year's Eve. I had a date and a party to go to. I was not sure exactly why, but as the evening went on, the feeling of nausea came over me. I fought it off and managed to get through the night but after getting home it progressively got worse.   Luckily the next day was Sunday and even if this was a touch of food poisoning or a simple stomach virus I could fend it off by Monday. No such luck. I called in sick and remained home. On Tuesday it got so bad I walked myself over to the nearest hospital in my neighborhood and went into the emergency room.

A tall middle-eastern Indian looking doctor walked in and began examining me. "Hello, my name is Dr. Patel. What seems to be the problem?"

"Well ever since like Saturday night, I went to this party and I started feeling really nauseated and it just keeps getting worse," I replied in pain.

Looking into my eyes he then says, "How long have you noticed that your eyes have been turning yellow?"

"Huh? Yellow?"

"I'm going to run some blood tests on you." He injected a needle into my arm to draw blood. "I'll be back in a little while."

I laid there on the emergency room gurney moaning from the constant nausea generating from my abdomen. Finally after what seemed like an eternity, Dr. Patel returned with another Indian looking doctor holding a clipboard and pen. Neither of them looked very happy.

"Michael, it looks like you have Hepatitis B."

"Huh? What was that?" I thought.

The other doctor chimed in. "Have you ever used intravenous drugs?" I was able to communicate a look of confusion through my painful grimaces.

"Drugs? What kind of drugs do you mean? You mean like shooting in the arm type stuff like heroin? Me? HELL NO!"

Although I had smoked marijuana while going to college in Cincinnati (as most college kids were doing at that time), once I had started practicing Buddhism I simply lost interest. It was never any sort of moral decision or even a conscious effort to stop. It just never occurred to me to do it anymore.

Then Dr. Patel stepped in. "Michael, have you had any sort of homosexual relationships?"

"What?"

"Well the reason why we are asking is that Hepatitis B is often associated with sharing drug needles and gay men who engage in anal sex," said the other doctor. "Are you sure?"

"Sure? Sure? What the hell are you guys talking about? I have never done needles and haven't so much as had the interest in holding the hand of another man let alone having anal sex with one!" But all I could think of is... *"Geez! How the HELL did I get this and do these guys even have to believe a word of what I'm saying?"*

Dr. Patel then said in an effort to calm me down, "Well although not common, it is possible to get it from eating bad seafood particularly things like raw clams although that's more common to Hepatitis A. We are going to need to keep you here at the hospital. Do you have someone you can call and bring over anything you might need?"

"What do we have to do?" I asked as panic started to settle in.

"We need to observe you," Dr. Patel said sadly. "Unfortunately while we have ways of preventing Hepatitis B, there is really no cure once you have it."

The next few days were pure hell. The nausea was so incredibly bad it was hard to get even two consecutive hours of sleep as I was constantly calling in a nurse to either give me a dose of Maalox or administer anti-nausea shots into my buttocks. The doctor would come in each day and press against my liver checking its swollenness and take more blood tests but it was only getting worse. I barely had enough energy to get to the bathroom where I would find myself pissing brown urine and crapping albino stools. I was in a bad way.

I was also getting tired of Dr. Patel's long sad face and dreaded more than anything the food cart coming around as I had to begin forcing food down my throat since nothing was appealing. Even if the disease didn't kill me directly, I could literally have starved myself to death because food was simply disgusting to me.

Finally after about four days of this and another discouraging report from Dr. Patel, I had to ask him where this was all going.

"Frankly Michael, we may need to start talking about life saving measures if this goes any further. I don't really have any good news for you. I'm sorry. The best I thing we can hope for is chronic Hepatitis. I say this in a sad way because you would have this in some form or another for the rest of your life. It's that bad I'm sorry. You certainly won't ever be able to drink alcohol anymore." (Not funny) "Your liver is taking a beating right now."

Life saving measures? Was I dying? How could this be? And even if I live, having a disease for the rest of my life? Would I be a carrier of the disease? That would certainly put an end to my social life!

At this point I felt there was only one option for me. I made a phone call to Jimmy who was coming to the hospital to visit me nearly every day traveling in from where he lived in Manhattan.

"Jimmy, it's me."

"Hey man, I'm coming over today. Probably around 2 PM."

"Listen man, I need you to do me a favor."

"Anything, what do you need?"

"Jimmy, I need you to stop by my apartment. Go into my bedroom and in my top dresser drawer you will find a little pouch that contains what looks like prayer beads and a small book with Chinese writing. Do you think you can get that and bring it over to me?"

"Yeah sure, no problem."

It was probably four years since I had uttered *Nam-myoho-renge-kyo* let alone recite the sutra portion of the practice which was part of the daily ceremony known as *Gongyo*. But as soon as Jimmy left the hospital I took out my sutra book and prayer beads, sat up in bed and began chanting. It was a struggle getting through that little sutra book as I had forgotten much of it but felt there were few choices left. The only cure available to me was my own life's ability to get my body to fight off the disease on its own. I mustered my determination by recalling all of the experiences I had with the practice prior to having faded away into the hell of marital turmoil and into the bliss of self absorbed egoism and nightly doses of New York's wide assortment of "meat" markets. During all this time, my Buddhist practice was non-existent.

I chanted, I grunted from pain, and I cried. Continuously facing hour upon hour of intense nausea, the abhorrence of food, and the fear that I might not even make it through this alive, I chanted as much as I possibly could.

Another two days passed with continuous digression and more bad news. But on the third day after I began chanting, Dr. Patel walked into my hospital room as he did almost every day but without the sullen face I had become so familiar with.

"Michael, I have some good news. It appears that your bilirubin count has gotten better. That's a good sign. It's still very high, but a move in the right direction. Let's check again tomorrow and see where we are at."

It felt like the first time I had a result from chanting when I damaged my father's car only this time it was my life. *"Yes,"* I again reminded myself, *"chanting works!"*

As soon as Dr. Patel left the room I immediately chanted as much as possible. Each day that went by saw my results getting better and better. So much better in fact that after 2 long weeks in the hospital I was permitted to return home although it would take another four weeks before I could return to work.

While I had not set up an altar or re-enshrine my *Gohonzon*, I continued to chant each day. I would normally just take the *Gohonzon* (still rolled up and in the original envelope I received it in), place it on top of my dresser and just chant to it that way.

In the meantime, I was going to Dr. Patel's office for regular checkups and blood tests. After about two months, Dr. Patel reported what to him was astonishing news.

"I can't believe this," he said while looking at my most recent blood test. "Your liver functions appear to be 100% back to normal. There is no trace of the disease. I'm amazed. You had one of the worst cases I had seen and at the very least you should have had chronic Hepatitis, but..." he started laughing, "you are like a medical miracle."

As though this were the most important question, I asked, "So I can drink?"

"Apparently so. I can't see any reason to tell you no. We'll continue doing tests. I would love to know how you kicked this so quickly."

I could have said because I chanted, but I just smiled and asked, "Maybe because I was in pretty good shape?"

"I don't know. I would love to keep running tests on you."

"Sure", I said with a smile feeling like Dr. Patel's prized specimen.

~~~

While I could never be certain how I originally got the disease, around three months prior to that New Year's Eve (which is usually about the period of time you carry the virus before it hits you), I recalled an incident that may have held the key. At a very popular disco club known as Heartbreak on Broadway in New York's SoHo area (which stands for "south of Houston St" pronounced "How-ston") and the one I frequented the most, I met a very pretty (Jewish) woman from Columbia.

Now when I say "Columbia" I don't mean Columbia University, I really mean the country Columbia which had the infamous label of being the world's capital exporter of cocaine. On our very first date she revealed to me that she was in fact a cocaine dealer trying to "get out of the game." She was very sexy, very pretty and I literally agreed to go along for the ride as we roamed Hells Kitchen Park in Manhattan in her Cadillac doing drug for money exchanges. On top of that, we made a stop at her Manhattan apartment where sitting around a wooden trunk with a hidden bottom panel, she pulled out what looked like a 2 pound brick of cocaine in front of 3 or 4 Columbian dudes in exchange for money.

I couldn't believe it. What if one of these guys was a cop or decided to get *gangsta'* on us and start shooting? I could see my poor Nana and mother reading it in the newspaper:

Young (Jewish) New York Man Gunned Down in Drug Deal

In an apparent drug for money exchange that went bad, Michael Friedman, a 29 year old studio engineer for NBC News, was killed by gunmen along with a young Columbian woman who was in the United States illegally and whose identity is being withheld by authorities. It's not clear what Friedman was doing at the mid-town apartment and police are investigating any criminal history Friedman may have been involved with.

Holy cow! Well needless to say, we consummated the relationship *before* leaving my apartment and *before* revealing to me her criminal profession. After my short one night career in a Columbian drug cartel, after dinner, and after being dropped back off at my apartment in Jackson Heights, I easily decided this was not a woman I would ever plan on marrying let alone DATE!

But a few days after returning home from the hospital I recollected a conversation I had with her that night. She told me about a breakup up she recently had with her fiancé. I recall her telling me he had been a drug addict who had gotten very sick! I don't even know how I had remembered that. The one and only date we had was more than three months prior to my getting ill. During the next few weeks following our date she tried calling me on several occasions only leaving me messages that I would not return until she finally *got* the message and stopped trying.

~~~

Shockingly and to my incredible delight, OUT OF NOWHERE while at home convalescing from a disease that nearly killed me, she called again! Almost four months since we went out on that date and I couldn't believe that she was calling me again!

"You're just the person I want to talk to!" I exclaimed as soon as she announced herself and said hello.

I'm not sure what her reaction was as for a moment she may have thought this was going to be good news and that I was going to ask to see her again.

"I just got home from the hospital about a week ago," as I continued. "I had a very serious case of Hepatitis B. I think I got it from you!"

At first there was silence but then she began sobbing, "The doctor told me I was not a carrier!"

Well apparently she was and her ex-boyfriend, an intravenous drug user, is where she got it from and passed it on to me. I had mixed emotions as I listened to her crying on the phone. I couldn't be sure whether to be angry or feel sorry for her.

"I'm sorry," I said somberly as she continued crying uncontrollably. "Forget it. Forget it. Please just forget it. It's over. It's OK."

"I'm so sorry," she said choking on her tears after which she just hung up the phone. I never heard from her again.

I can't imagine how low and cursed she must have felt. It was really a very sad moment.

I would return to work just before I would be forced into workman's comp and have my pay cut in half. I continued chanting (although in an abbreviated version) but which did not include setting up another altar, re-enshrining my Gohonzon or getting in touch with NSA. So for the next couple of years, things returned back to "normal." I was dating again but with more of an interest in finding a stable relationship while trying my best to avoid any possible one night stands. One such relationship would change the course of my life and Buddhist practice until this day.

~~~

I started dating Diane, a young nurse who worked at Lexington Hospital in mid-town Manhattan. Things seemed to be going quite well. I had a very pretty professional girlfriend, a great job, and was in even better shape than ever as I began 9 months of training for the annual stair climbing race up the Empire

State Building. All seemed fantastic when suddenly my nurse girlfriend began acting a little strange towards me. We agreed to stop seeing each other when she began getting angry with me at the drop of a pin which started a very quick downspin.

Life went on, but about a month later Diane calls me up.

"Hey Diane, what's going on?"

"Well, Michael I feel really bad about how things turned out. I know I wasn't treating you very well and that wasn't very fair of me."

"Hey, yeah... Diane whatever... I couldn't figure out what I had done," I replied.

She took a deep breath, "The truth is, I was talking to one of the doctors about you. I had mentioned that you had Hepatitis B before we met." Then taking a long pause she says to me, "Hepatitis B patients are also among the most prone to also having AIDS. And so when he told me that, I got a little scared and began freaking out a little."

My heart began to race. *AIDS?*

"Anyway," she went on, "I just felt I needed to tell you that and perhaps suggest you might consider getting tested."

In the mid-80's when AIDS first began rearing its ugly head, it was considered strictly a gay or needle using disease and after we hung up I just shrugged it off. But as the next week or so went by, her words kept echoing in my mind... *"Hepatitis B patients are also among the most prone to also having AIDS."*

Finally I couldn't stand it any longer and decided to make a phone call to Dr. Patel.

"Dr. Patel, I know this is more about paranoia than anything else, but you see I was dating this nurse who told me...", as I continued with the story, "...and so thought it would be a good idea if I had an AIDS test."

At the time, AIDS testing had not been perfected and could sometimes read inaccurately. So Dr. Patel told me he was willing to do it, but warned me that if it came back positive, there was not much I could do with the information. None-the-less, I needed to get it off my mind as I was also beginning to feel some sort of cold or flu virus come on which only added to my paranoia. So I went to get the blood test.

About a day or so later Dr. Patel calls me.

"Michael, I don't know how to tell you this, but it appears you have AIDS."

My heart and everything below dropped to the floor. "What?"

"I'm sorry, I'm very sorry."

"Dr. Patel. That's impossible!"

"You had gay relations, did you not?"

"What? No!" Apparently the other doctor that interviewed me along with Dr. Patel decided to make me a homosexual in order to diagnose the reason I contracted Hepatitis B! But this time Dr. Patel could sense I wasn't just baffled by the notion of being gay, I was now quite angry.

"Well," Dr. Patel said with a bit of confusion, "Let me look further into this, but these are the results. I will call you again if I have any other information. You might want to consider another test."

I was shaking as I hung up the phone. AIDS meant certain death at the time. After battling a disease that almost killed me, I now was dealt with another disease that in all certainty *would* kill me. Once again, I had to turn to Buddhism.

I decided it was time to bring out the BIG guns. I needed to enshrine my *Gohonzon*. I needed to do it right, and I needed to do it now! With plenty of time left before I had to be at the studio for work, I immediately left my Jackson Heights apartment and headed straight for the number 7 train to Flushing, Queens. While fighting back tears I headed straight to a Buddhist paraphernalia store near the temple that sold such things as altars and all the accoutrements.

By the time I got back, I still had another hour or so left before I had to leave again and get into Manhattan for work. I found a table, set up my altar with my newly purchased *butsudan* (a box with doors that holds the *Gohonzon*), candle sticks, water cup, a bell, incense burner, and cut greens. I was ready. I carefully removed my rolled up *Gohonzon* from the envelope I had originally received it in nearly 11 years earlier in Cleveland. I slowly untied the string that kept it fastened in a roll and carefully hung it inside the *butsudan*.

Sitting on the floor I gazed upon this scroll that felt like a long lost friend I had ignored for years. I was overwhelmed with more emotion as I began crying almost uncontrollably while trying to chant through the tears.   Once I had returned home from the hospital I limited my practice to just chanting *Nam-myoho-renge-kyo* (called *daimoku*) but refrained from actually doing any sort of "formal" practice.   More importantly, any chanting I did was either to the envelope containing the *Gohonzon* that I placed on top of my dresser or when I really got lazy to the dresser drawer itself where the *Gohonzon* rested for years.

My hands were shaking as I continued chanting when finally I rang the bell to begin reciting the sutra.   I lifted the small book to my eyes filled with tears while holding my prayer beads between my fingers.   I began...

"Myoho Renge Kyo... Hoben pon dai ni, niji sesson ju san mai anjo nikki go sharihotsu sho but chie..." all the way through the entire book and then back again following the prescribed format that we did at the time.   Once I completed that portion and still with about 15 minutes left before I needed to leave for work, I started chanting *daimoku* for about another 5 minutes.   I rang the bell and recited in my mind the last "silent" prayer in the back of the book.   Looking up at the *Gohonzon*, I completed the first *Gongyo* I had done in nearly four years by ringing the bell and slowly chanting *Nam-myoho-renge-kyo* three last times to officially end the ceremony.

I bowed my head and took a deep breath.   As though on cue, my phone started ringing.   I got up to answer.

"Hello?"

"Michael, it's Dr. Patel."

"Hi doctor."

"Listen Michael," his voice sounded like he was about to cry himself as he paused a moment causing my heart to skip. "A mistake was made. Your blood test is fine. It was not your test that I was referring to. Your test was negative, you don't have AIDS."

Perhaps he thought I would be angry for having made this mistake and giving me the scare of my life. Perhaps he was shocked when instead what I wanted to do was reach through the phone and hug him with all my heart. I was overjoyed! More importantly, as soon as I hung up the phone with Dr. Patel, I ran into my bedroom sat once more in front of my *Gohonzon* and this time with tears of joy chanted *Nam-myoho-renge-kyo* three times vowing that I would never again doubt the power of this practice and that I would never again quit. From that day on, I never did.

~~~

My Buddhist practice had been broken off due to the machinations of the Nichiren Shoshu priesthood whose shenanigans would continue even to the point where the entire international lay organization would eventually sever their relationship. In fact it may very well go down as the largest ex-communication event in the history of religion when around 1991 the head temple of Nichiren Shoshu led by high priest Nikken Abe expelled over 12 million lay believers of Soka Gakkai International worldwide. It was big news in Japan but hardly a blip on the screen here in the United States. This incident however may one day become a precedent of a growing revolution in man's relationship to his faith particularly where religious leaders find purpose and what purpose we find in them.

There perhaps is no authority more dangerous than those with ties to our religious beliefs. It seems no wonder therefore that by their clear perspective, the authors of the United States Constitution designated separation of church and state as its very first amendment. For the most part the world had never really known civil governments free of religious attachment until the advent of our constitution. Of course many governments would eventually follow suit, but this is often taken for granted and perhaps not seen as part of a significant spiritual evolutionary process among human beings.

The heart of a religious leader can easily find conflict between what would seem to be the purpose of his role in religious guidance based upon the teachings of any one religion to one of divine dominium over the lives of lay practitioners. I dare say that this balance all too often has swung in the wrong direction.

Humanity has always been filled with suffering and death. Without exception, the founder of every religion had the interest of the people's well-being in mind and attempted (in their own way) to help end human suffering. Human beings however will suffer as long as the most pondering questions remain unanswered: Where did I come from? What happens after I die? Why do we suffer? What is life's purpose? Regardless of the arguments of how religions become skewed from the intent of their founders, the questions surrounding life and death, or rather the "truths" they endorsed become powerful matters of faith. It always comes back to the *death view*. Unfortunately, fear often becomes the bi-product of faith once faith becomes an impervious reality in one's mind. Fear is without a doubt the most susceptible human emotion that allows those in religious authority to control groups of people. Even our own government has been successfully employing these tactics.

Be it the robe, the collar, the ordination, or the habit, they become invitations to crawl up upon pedestals of assumed virtue and along with that, the illusion that these ordinary human beings are for some reason the intermediaries between this life and the next. While governments may attempt to control by law or shear force the will of the people, there is nothing more effectual than the uncertainty of an eternity held in check by the religious arbiter.

I have no bitterness towards Tono who in 1980 caused the confusion in New York which eventually led to the abandonment of my own Buddhist practice nor even Nikken Abe whose envy for power helped create perhaps the largest group of lay believers in the history of religion to become completely devoid of clergy. Instead, there is a new found freedom. We have been unshackled by centuries of humankind's delusion of "priestly" religious eminence.

I am not suggesting that there is no place in society for religious leadership and particularly in spiritual guidance. There are after all, many role models (past and present) who not by virtue of their position, but by their virtuous deeds demonstrate the way to live based upon religious influence. Mother Teresa comes to mind as well as Gandhi. The Reverend Martin Luther King and the man I consider my own mentor in the art of human living, Daisaku Ikeda are examples of such individuals.

As I think back to my elation upon the announcement of a priest coming to New York, I have to reflect on just how naïve was the source of that jubilation. The mere fact that a man in robe was coming to our area immediately brought about a sense that we would be blessed with a person of extra-special quality. I'm sure it would be no different had we been Jews practicing for years deprived of a synagogue and Rabbi or Christians having no church, priest or minister. These men after all are supposedly our theological experts who deliver sermons in houses blessed as havens upon which we are able to exorcise our demons and become better individuals or at least find our salvation.

The truth in fact is that there are no levels of knowledge or spiritual rankings reserved for members of clergy. These centuries' old assumptions however are beginning to crumble before our very eyes. Goodness aside, there are far too many examples throughout history where men ordained by religious authority have used their supposed superior status for their own personal gain and self preservation. Many of them don't even want to consider what they do as categorized a "profession." Even that word is beneath many of them. Professions are what lay people engage in but not priests, monks, rabbis, ministers, pastors, imams, mullahs, or Brahmins. Perhaps they would rather you consider what they do as their burden. Professions are chosen and burdens are not.

While it may sound like I'm calling for the abolishment of any and all clergy, frankly I actually have no opinion as to whether they can or should continue any role in world religion or spirituality. On the other hand, I would easily admit that I'm advocating the continued empowerment of lay believers and if their clergy can survive that awakening so be it. But if they should slowly begin fading away because of that, so be it as well.

~~~

The Sho-Shinkai incident was quelled some time around 1980 and Nikken Abe was able to maintain his challenged position as high priest of Nichiren Shoshu. At the same time, the lay organization of Soka Gakkai in Japan was able to carry on its own semblance of peace with the clergy in spite of 50 tumultuous years between both sides. The relationship with the Nichiren Shoshu priesthood was more a matter of circumstance rather than choice.

The defeat of Japan's imperial military and their surrender in 1945 would bring about desperate times for millions of Japanese. It was from here that the Soka Gakkai emerged guided by the second president of the organization, Josei Toda after his release from a Japanese prison. Toda and his mentor Tsunesaburo Makiguchi had been imprisoned as "thought criminals" because of their opposition to the government's religion policies just before the onset of the war and where Makiguchi would die a martyr's death. Upon his own release after 2 years of imprisonment, Toda began an inexorable Buddhist movement within Japan's war torn society.

Unlike the prosperity enjoyed by the victorious United States after the war, Japan was filled with the poor, the hungry, the homeless, and the sick. At the same time, they were also introduced to a new freedom after their defeat and American occupation: freedom of religion. As a result, many religions both new and old, "cult" and traditional, native and foreign, began proselytizing to get a foothold in society (including Christianity), but none as successfully as the Soka Gakkai who preached the philosophy and practices of the 13th century Japanese Buddhist priest, Nichiren Daishonin.

The Soka Gakkai was founded by educator Tsunesaburo Makiguchi who around 1930, was seeking to revise the Japanese educational system which like society and the government itself was overtly proud, uncompassionate, rigid, and totalistic. In seeking schools of philosophical thought that would support his efforts, he came across the teachings of Nichiren who was himself a revolutionary having remonstrated with both government and religious authorities nearly costing him his life on several occasions. It was a peril that Makiguchi himself would not escape.

The middle aged Makiguchi was impressed with Nichiren's teachings and practice that emphasized the equality of all human beings and their equal ability to attain what to most (or even all) other Buddhist teachings claim to be impossible in a single lifetime; the condition of enlightenment. Nichiren taught the ideal of creating value with one's life which ultimately would lead to this kind of happiness uninfluenced by external circumstances. Rules and rigidity dictated by religions or by government were to Nichiren the obvious wrong answers to a 13th century society plagued with death, despair, and the potential of foreign invasions... conditions that would return to Japan over 600 years later.

While several Nichiren "sects" would splinter off after his death in 1282, a small group of priests known as Nichiren Shoshu claimed to have had direct lineage with Nichiren and his key disciple Nikko Shonin who after the death of his teacher, not only continued his mentors effort to reform society while remonstrating with the authorities, but was determined to preserve Nichiren's writings, the integrity of his teachings, and his prescriptive Buddhist practice. Actually, Nikko knew nothing about "Nichiren Shoshu" (a name they came up with in 1912) but instead referred to his mentor's teachings as the Fuji School after he established a temple known as Taiseki-ji near Mount Fuji.

Over the centuries that would follow after Nikko's death, the priests of Taiseki-ji would eventually end their perceptively "bad" attitudes with the government and religious authorities and instead simply became a mere secluded small fraternity of priests. But their possession of Taiseki-ji, many of the original writings of Nichiren himself (still preserved in his hand writing today) and in particular an object Nichiren had inscribed in wood known as the *Dai-Gohonzon* (which established a blue print for the inscription of individual *Gohonzons*), made them a key player in Nichiren Buddhism. Makiguchi became a practitioner himself, authored a proposal for educational reform titled Education for Creative Living, and in 1932 created his own lay organization mainly made up of fellow educators and students known as Soka Kyoiku Gakkai (Value Creation Education Society).

But as war approached and the Japanese became more militaristic, in an attempt to draw society into a united effort the government employed their infamous Maintenance of Public Order Act. Among other things, it was dictated by the government that Shinto would become the national religion. While they were not trying to abolish other religions, they demanded that all religious groups and establishments accept a Shinto talisman in recognition of their edict.

In spite of Nichiren and Nikko's spirit of never succumbing to any sort of compromise, the priests of Nichiren Shoshu easily accepted the order to avoid confrontation with the government. Makiguchi on the other hand refused and voiced his opposition not only to the talisman but to Japan's war efforts and their alliance with Nazi Germany. He and several other members of Soka Kyoiku Gakkai were placed in prison as "thought criminals" and where in 1944 at the age of 73 he died from abuses and deprivation.

Josei Toda some 30 years younger considered Makiguchi his mentor and remained in prison until his own release in 1945 after more than two years in prison and only two weeks before the end of the war. But while in prison, Toda studied and practiced Nichiren Buddhism relentlessly in spite of his isolation from his family and uncertainty of what would be the outcome of the war.

Determined not only to reform education but society as a whole, Toda changed the name of Soka Kyoiku Gakkai to Soka Gakkai (Value Creation Society) and embarked on an intense and vigorous movement to introduce Nichiren Buddhism to his war torn country. In the context of what Japan was after World War II, Toda felt he had little choice in how aggressive he needed to be in spreading Nichiren Buddhism and growing the Soka Gakkai. Industry was broken and people were sick, poor, and homeless. From only a handful of members left after the war, by 1958 when Toda died (after never really being in very good health after his experience in prison), the Soka Gakkai grew to 750,000 families in Japan after only 13 years and today over 10,000,000 Japanese families and one of if not *the* largest form of organized religion in Japan.

Just before his death, Toda called upon a young man named Daisaku Ikeda to spread this Buddhism and the Soka Gakkai outside of Japan. Instrumental in the Japanese movement during the 1950's, Ikeda considered Toda his own mentor as Toda considered Makiguchi. Ikeda would become the third president of the Soka Gakkai and eventually president of the international organization Soka Gakkai International as the organization spread out into 127 countries and nearly another 2 million Nichiren Buddhist practitioners. In actuality, the members of SGI (and NSA in America) were never really members of the Nichiren Shoshu temple itself but rather two completely separate cooperating entities. In a sense the priesthood was able to shackle the lay organization by the perception of who is rightly endowed with the ability to inscribe and issue to practitioners the great heirloom of Nichiren's philosophy which is the *Gohonzon* itself. In this way the priesthood was able to keep hostage the lay believers because of this presumption as well as the fact that they hold many original precious and priceless artifacts from Nichiren himself dating back almost 800 years.

But up until the growth of the Soka Gakkai, this priesthood had been nothing but a small band of poor priests living quietly and humbly near the base of Mount Fuji nearly starving after World War II. Within a very short time however and because of the explosive growth of the Soka Gakkai, these priests grew in numbers by the dozens. As a result, they began demanding large financial donations from the lay organization that included the building of new temples throughout Japan and the other countries. This included one of the greatest architectural structures ever built known as Sho-Hondo and which housed the *Dai-Gohonzon* which was carved by Nichiren in 1282 (or at his bequest) and one year and a day before his death.

And so the drama was set. The Nichiren Shoshu priesthood and in particular their leader Nikken Abe, were growing more and more frustrated about their position as priests without also being the leaders of all lay members. In spite of the fact that huge sums of money were flowing into the clergy because of the sincere donations made by the SGI membership, they were not really in control of the believers themselves. Furthermore SGI began asking unwelcome questions regarding the increasing decedent lifestyles of some of these priests along with rumors of Nikken Abe's own plan to build an elaborate private retirement home for himself that included an indoor swimming pool. Considering the price of land in Japan, the project was rumored to be in the millions. And I don't mean Yen.

It seemed that many of these priests were literally out of control. More importantly there was talk that many of them were not really even practicing Buddhism very regularly.

Before you simply view this as just another tired secretive and sorted story of corruption within a religious organization, like pedophile priests, money laundering, sexually permissive ministers including the hypocrisy of closeted homosexuals, please bear in mind the differences. To protect their position and potentially soiled character, they actually banned anyone associated with the Soka Gakkai from the grounds of all temples including the head temple itself with its many priceless artifacts that are treasures to all practitioners of Nichiren Buddhism around the world. In addition, by banning Soka members from the "benefits' of priestly association, they also declared that no Soka members were eligible to receive *Gohonzon* without disavowing their association with SGI. However, a group of priests sympathetic to SGI came into possession of a *Gohonzon* tablet inscribed in 1720 by the high priest Nichikan.

Considered one of the great scholars and protectors of the orthodoxy of this Buddhism, the tablet was handed over to SGI. Now the Soka Gakkai was able to issue *Gohonzons* to lay believers without the need of a priest.

The priesthood actually placed itself in between a person and the ultimate goal of the religion's ideals. But in 1991 over 12 million stood fast with the awareness that no one with a title of any kind can stand between the ultimate principles of a religion and a person who practices it. But such has been the tendency of clergy for centuries. The pious few have been feeding upon the faith and superstitions of ordinary people throughout the ages.

~~~

I know I'm guilty of generalizing. Clergy in and of itself is not evil anymore than government. The question I raise is one of purpose. We can think of dozens of reasons why we need government in spite of the potential for great wrongdoing there as well. The common denominator between the two is that they are suppose to serve their constituent or congregations, but the potential for the reverse is far stronger with persons in religious authority. In America, while government at all levels is not immune to corruption and foul play by any means, at least there are checks and balances. Whether we take the process for granted and use it, there are elections. The parties of clerics on the other hand, create their own hierarchy and are really not obliged to anyone, except perhaps some higher order like God for example.

Clergies often take on autocratic structures and even monarchies where family members pass the torch and inherit power from one generation to the next. And while they don't have armies, history has shown that through their mutual and beneficial alliances with governments, military actions have been supported or influenced by religious goals generated from within clerical parties. Hence even more reason why our founding fathers placed separation of church and state at the very top of the list.

The seriousness and historical depth of collaborations between religion and government goes far beyond whether our children need an opportunity for a religious moment in school or whether the Ten Commandments needs to be displayed as the moral groundwork of our courts. It comes down to having a firewall against the great potential evil created by clerical/political pacts.

This is part of the great maturation of humanity and one which I experienced on a personal level. It's not a matter of whether clergy should exist or not. Rather, it must come to the point where we realize that there is nothing extraordinary or superior about a man who has chosen the path of religious vocation. There are many among them of noble intention with good hearts and unselfish ambition. But whether religious guidance and encouragement comes from a priest or an auto mechanic, both have equal standing as species of human beings with neither one having any inside track on the truth.

Chapter 6

Dependent Origination

M y AIDS scare was a pretty solid wake up call. For over 2 years, I never stopped chanting on a consistent daily basis sometimes as much as 2 hours per day. In spite of this fact, I was still not involved with the Buddhist lay organization and had not been for over six years since Tono and the Shoshin-Kai priest incident 7 years earlier that nearly wiped out the organization in New York City.

In June of 1987 after returning from a Colorado white water rafting trip, I came back to find out that the negotiations between my union (NABET) and NBC were not going very well on new contract talks. We voted to give our union officials the power to call a strike and soon afterward that's exactly what they did.

Unprepared, I found myself assigned to a picket line in front of 30 Rockefeller Plaza in New York City.

Running low on funds and with plenty of extra time on my hands, my life once more seemed to be floating along uncertain paths. To exacerbate the situation even more, NBC sold the Radio Network (along with the show I had been working on for over six years) to Westwood One which meant that once the strike was over, I was heading to a position in television yet to be determined.

Chanting before my altar was what continued to give me hope and strength but at the same time, I felt that I needed to go further. At the very least I needed to hear other voices chanting besides my own. Truth in fact, I felt I could use a little spiritual and moral support. I contacted NSA with a clear arrangement in mind that the only organizational activity I would be willing to participate in was chanting. No conventions, no propagation activities, and no organizational responsibilities. I just wanted the community of chanters and nothing more.

The Organized Community of Believers

Organized religions have taken a pretty bad rap for many decades and for good reason. They are often corrupt at their highest levels, they often bend the philosophies of their teachings to suit their own needs, they often seek conformity over unity because in conformity they can more easily have power over their followers, and many have become huge centers of financial revenue under the guise of non-profit.

Of course we count on organization in almost every aspect of our lives both natural (like eco-systems and our own bodily functions working in unison), as well as man made institutions like governments and education. The alternative is chaos. And even if *every* government were corrupt and *every* educational system ineffective, that wouldn't mean we could function without them. It would only mean we would have to continue to work to correct the problems because we need both to advance and live together within a social structure.

Organized religion on the other hand is amassed with grey area since one might still dispute that we don't need religion let alone an organization to support it. Of course I can't argue with the nay-sayers who reject religion completely and don't recognize it as one of mankind's three evolutionary processes. Since I'm not a scientist, I can't explain the details behind the causes and logic of physical evolution yet we know it has happened and is continuing to happen. It is a progression that involves and is related to the systematic processes of nature's organized eco-system and nature's adaptation to its continuing changes. Techno/scientific evolution results from our innate need as a species to always improve and advance be it government systems, scientific understanding of our physical surroundings (both inner space and outer space), and require man made organizations to advance. Yet for some reason we might believe that religion or rather the spiritual evolution of our species can somehow advance without it.

Let's say you believe in God as at least 90% of Americans claim they do[6]. Unless you invented the God concept yourself, you are already connected to organized religion. Whether you like it or not, your belief in God is linked to a community of religious belief that caused you to believe in God in the first place. Even if you don't belong to any formalized religious institution and refuse to do so, you inherited or adapted the God concept *from* organized institutions of religious belief. Maybe you don't belong to the Catholic Church, but your parents did, or their parents did, or their grandparents did, but I can guarantee you that someone along your line did in fact "belong." So while you can deny your own affiliations, you cannot deny your lineage to it. So if you'll agree that the one-God concept is a spiritual advancement over Zeus then you can't disagree that it took a community of like minded believers to advance that concept. Religion therefore advances within and via community.

But how organized is organized? Does it require any sort of hierarchical system with officials and leaders? Does it require a clergy? Well here is a reality check to answer the question. I know that I would never have been introduced to Buddhism had it not been for the American lay organization known then as NSA (Nichiren Shoshu of America) and now known as SGI-USA (Soka Gakkai International-USA). Whether I reject being part of an organization or not, this is an undeniable fact. Was it necessary therefore that in order

---

[6] Harris Poll #11, February 26, 2003

for me to have ever practiced Buddhism that a formally organized group of practitioners exist?   How can I say no?

My conclusion therefore is that in order for people to practice religion, any religion (unless self made), organization is required to advance it and for one very important reason; the community of believers themselves.   The administration of any organization should always be for that purpose only.   Unfortunately there is a fine and dangerous line between whose purposes are being served.   Historically, organized religious groups have an abysmal record of crossing the line onto the side favoring the administrators of the organization itself.   It's no wonder that there is so much cynicism in the world regarding organized religion.   Of course the same can be said of governments particularly before the birth of the United States to where, as in his Gettysburg address, Abraham Lincoln described our government as, *"...of the people, by the people, for the people..."* prior to which all governments throughout the world perhaps without exception were institutions of the government, by the government, and for the government.

American democracy and our concept of freedom are not even three centuries old.   When you compare that to a world ruled for thousands of years by a variety of dictators and monarchies, we should be in awe of the fact that the founding fathers of our country were not too cynical to believe that government was flawed by its very existence.   Since power and egoism are inherent evils of man, organized religion is not inherently evil, but like governments easily inherited by evil. Since we cannot deny the need for government and as I believe, deny the need for spiritual growth, then we must continue to right the wrong as our founding fathers did and as we must also do with religion. While they are necessary in creating congruity among believers, there should always be a little bit of guarded skepticism even when we consider organizations that are led and coordinated by non-ordained lay leaders.

~~~

Not long after I went back to my first meeting in July of 1987, NSA was embarking in what was a traditional August campaign to introduce as many people as possible to the practice of Buddhism even if it meant going out on the street to talk to total strangers just as they had done after the war in Japan (and which method of introduction would end in 1991). When I went to my very first meeting at Christy's apartment in Cleveland I found NSA to be a bit overwhelming which was why I had kept it at arm's length until many of the members forced the organization (at least in New York City) into a much softer phase. But the growth of membership also flattened out and along with the Shoshin-kai priest problem in the late 70's, George Williams who was the NSA General Director at the time, was pushing for the organization to return to its more intense beginnings which was one of the reasons I didn't hang in.

And so while I knew this was the organization I was returning to, I once again was reminding everyone of why I left in the first place and what I was willing and not willing to do. Chanting with everyone... yes... going out on the streets of Manhattan and talking to perfect strangers in an attempt to invite them to a Buddhist introductory meeting... no.

~~~

NSA found its roots mainly in Japanese women who began coming to the United States after marrying American military servicemen in the 1950's and early 1960's. Many of these marriages ended up failing as a result of cultural differences, language barriers, and men probably too young to handle it themselves. Some of these young women had already been members of the Soka Gakkai in Japan or began taking up the practice either because of their parents who were members themselves in Japan or influenced by other newly imported Japanese compatriots.

While the organization in Japan would slowly tone down its intense approach towards Buddhist proselytization as it found a strong foothold in Japanese society, it was under these conditions that the Japanese war brides of American GI's began spreading this Buddhism to Americans. The first General Director, Masayasu Sadanaga (a young Japanese immigrant who would take on the very American name George M. Williams), were products of the Japanese Soka Gakkai movement of the 1950's and all that went along with it. More to the point, it became a 1950's Japanese movement with intense propagation activities under predominantly Japanese American leadership all the way up until 1991 when Daisaku Ikeda (President of Soka Gakkai International) removed George Williams of his responsibilities.   On the one hand, you could argue that these homesick native Japanese Americans were selfishly creating an organization that best suited their culture or that in spite of their incredible determination and pure motives, simply didn't know any better.   I believe it was a bit of both.   But putting a stop to activities such as on-the-street introductions or the large challenging   conventions   the   organization   would periodically arrange, Ikeda demanded that the members practice and introduce Buddhism to society not as though we were 1947 war weary Japanese, but as Americans suitable to the diverse cultures of the United States.   The Japanese method worked somewhat in the 60's and 70's where with such things as Vietnam, drugs, and Watergate, America had its own problems.   The youth of America was willing to experiment and look outside the box of the "establishment" and NSA experienced a pretty rapid growth itself during that time albeit nothing like Japan.

~~~

But it wasn't 1991 yet.   It was 1987 and still the organization of Japanese American immigrants and one still associated with the Nichiren Shoshu clergy.   It would have been one thing to walk out on the street and talk to depressed down trodden Japanese who had just come out of a defeated war, (not to mention having a couple of atom bombs dropped on it).   It might have even been another if it were 1968 where instead of finding New York filled with career climbing Reagan era Yuppies (young urban professionals) we would be able to entice LSD popping free loving Hippies.

At these August (and February) introductory meetings we would chant normally from 7:00 PM until 7:30 PM and then go out and do what was called street *geishu*. A Japanese term like so many that could have been easily translated into English in those days, simply meant random introductions to total strangers and an effort to get a guest to come to a meeting. Evident that we were assimilating ourselves to Japanese terminology, community centers were known as *kai-kans* and organizational positions of leadership were known as *chos* (pronounced like "chose"). Instead of simply saying "yes" we said "*hai*." We sang Japanese songs in Japanese fashion. You didn't just introduce someone to Buddhism, you *shakabuku'd* them; pronounced like "shock-a-bookoo." (I had always wondered who these poor little bookoo creatures were and why these Buddhists were so interested in shocking them. It was all a bit weird.)

But in spite of the fact that NSA seemed to be teetering on what to an outsider might be considered a "cult," I felt very comfortable around the members not to mention that the membership had grown dramatically in the nearly seven years since I had left. I think the main reason I felt this way was because of how normal everyone really was in spite of the "Japanification" of the organization. The membership was made up of people from all walks of life including lawyers, doctors, educators, students, working and aspiring Broadway actors and actresses, sales people, and at least one broadcasting employee out on strike. (Well make that two since I also introduced my best friend Jimmy to Buddhism and who started practicing himself.)

As I made plainly clear, I was willing to sit at the meetings and chant, even participate in the meeting, but walking out on the street (especially on hot sticky New York nights) with a pamphlet explaining *Nam-myoho-renge-kyo* and the benefits of Buddhism to a total stranger was just too creepy for me. Oh the images of Hare Krishna and Moonies! But that was until shortly after when I met May, another member at a Buddhist meeting.

It was certain that my karma was not only my weakness regarding women, but the fortune of being able to benefit from it. My first Buddhist meeting was secondary 12 years earlier to the objective of getting a date with Christy. In the same way, May would also lead me into another phase of my practice in the organization.

May's looks reminded me of one of my favorite actresses, Susan Hayward (although a bit before my time). Like Hayward, May carried the same sort of mature and sophisticated beauty that was reminiscent of the late Hollywood star right down to her full head of medium long brown wavy hair, and striking blue eyes. Taking into consideration that May was also a Buddhist, made her extraordinarily inviting.

It was now 7:30 PM and the bell rang ending the chanting. A middle aged attorney named Roger who was the "sho-bucho" (chapter coordinator) immediately sprang up. Somewhat short and a bit gawky, Roger compensated for his 50 something age surrounded in a room of 20 and 30 something members by displaying the most vigorousness and biggest smile in the room often to the point of awkwardness.

"OK," he said clenching his fists and gesturing with his arms, "let's go out and find someone who will not only want to come to our meeting this evening but who will be encouraged to practice this Buddhism and want to receive their own Gohonzon!" While looking at his watch he then said, "It's a little after 7:30 now, so let's meet back here at 8:00. How does that sound, OK?"

"Hai," several people shouted!

As members began standing up and moving toward the door I remained seated as usual.

"Michael, you're staying here, right?" Roger politely asked as he passed by.

"Uhhhhh yeah…."

"No, come out with us," said a soft pleading voice that was May's as she stood near the door about to exit. "We'll have fun. You'll see. Come on."

I looked at May. She was ravishing.

"OK, what the hell. Why not."

Roger was shocked. "Well that's great!"

Even Sara, Rogers's petite 19 year old daughter chimed in while giggling. "Wow," as she looked back and forth between May and myself.

"Well," said Roger beaming, "It must be you May, because Michael has been here on several occasions and has never gone out to do street geishu! Congratulations May, congratulations Michael!"

Oh brother, how embarrassing! The word "congratulations" was used for almost everything. If you said you received a new job... congratulations! If you said you lost your job...congratulations! I think it once again goes back to the limited English that the Japanese members in America had in finding the closest English word that might match what they were trying to express. I grabbed some pamphlets and proceeded out the door following May.

So there I was strolling out on a warm humid Manhattan evening looking for any passersby to approach.

"OK", I asked May, "how do we do this?"

May just smiled back at me about to answer when a young man in his 20's carrying a backpack was about to pass by. May jumped over to him.

"Hi, have you ever heard of *Nam-myoho-renge-kyo*?"

I moved closer to where I could hear what she was saying.

"Huh, what's that?" replied the smiling young man who was obviously a bit uncomfortable for having stopped once May abruptly invaded his space.

"Well, it's a Buddhist chant and you can chant for anything you want. What's your name?"

"No, I don't think so," replied the young man.

"Oh come on. Why don't you just stop over to hear about it?" pleaded May.

"I really have to be somewhere."

I'm sure while the guy was trying to say no and move on, he must have also been wondering what the very pretty May, professionally dressed and adorned with makeup, (rather than in a sari with some florescent line painted down her forehead holding a flower) would be doing out here proselytizing religion. She handed him a pamphlet and started pointing things out to him.

"I'm sure you've heard of Tina Turner, right? Well that's her, she also chants. And while millions of people chant in Japan, we are introducing this to America and you really should stop by. It's really incredible."

The young man took a big sigh looking down the street as though he might find some other excuse to get out of this. "What is this exactly?"

"It's a Buddhist chant and you can really chant for anything you want! Oh come on. We're just around the corner and will just take a few minutes."

He started thinking about it staring at the pamphlet. May kept pushing, "Fifteen minutes that's all. It will change your life. Is there anything you might like to change about your situation right now?"

"Well sure, of course," he replied while retaining his somewhat obligatory smile.

"Then come on," May said once again as she began shifting her weight to walk towards the apartment where we were holding the meeting.

"OK," he replied as his smile faded. "But just for 15 minutes."

"Great," exclaimed May as he began to follow her. "My name is May and this is Michael. What's your name?"

Caring For People Outside the Tribe

Jesus was a Jew who at some point decided that the "love" of a single God and the commandments taught in the Jewish teachings were not meant for Jews alone, but for all human beings. The idea of stepping outside the "tribe" and converting non-Jews into the single God concept was extremely radical to the Jewish way of thinking. Furthermore, he began talking in such a way that would not only challenge the beliefs and rituals of Judaism, but the entire Roman Empire.

To the ruling powers he became a seditious threat and to many Jews a royal pain in the ass. For Jesus was stirring up the pot by preaching the imminent coming of God's reign and the need for mankind to repent and accept. In order to accomplish this, it would appear that according to the New Testament, Jesus was trying to convince people to embrace such things as brotherly love and the purification of one's heart by ending such thoughts as lust, hostility, and the pursuit of wealth and power. This to him was far more important than mere ritualism. And while it's historically unfounded that anyone thought of him as the prophetic messiah during his lifetime, there is no doubt that his radical movement which really took greater hold after his execution, was pivotal to western history and a reflection of mankind's spiritual evolution.

But perhaps while betrayed, Jesus was a Jew who died a Jew. The movement to carry his message would a century later come to be known as Christianity once he had been deemed the messiah long after his death.   (Christ as meaning the Lord's Anointed or Messiah.)   However, in spite of the fact that this was essentially a Jewish movement, the entirety of the Jewish community was not convinced and much of it continued as it always had.

The Jews began spreading out all over Eastern Europe, Western Europe, and eventually both North and South America including the United States often because they were simply chased from one place to the next.   The adage "wandering Jew" which even became the name of a house plant reflected a history that for centuries and until the advent of modern Israel is reflective of a people who really never had any foundation of religious-politico position.   Instead, Jews would set up communities in various nations.

In addition and sometimes to their own demise, Jews come from a long tradition of education that probably finds its roots in the arduous demand placed particularly on Jewish males to study sacred scriptures such as the Torah and Kabbalah. While not given any sort of governmental powers due to prejudice, once Jews assimilated in society they would often would raise themselves up in professional fields unfettered by political ambitions like science, business, and medicine. As a result, despots like Hitler used not only anti-Semitic sympathies, but enhanced it by playing on the social envy of Jewish success.

Although somewhat tapered down compared to my grandparents and even great-grandparents, the Jewish tradition was very much alive and well in my childhood. To the best of her ability while living in the predominantly white Italian Catholic middle-class blue collar neighborhood of Mayfield Heights, Ohio, my mother was pretty passionate about keeping the precepts of her own strict Jewish upbringing. She was adamant about using only kosher foods, had separate plates and silverware for meat and dairy, sent me to Hebrew school to be bar-mitzvah'd (which I was at age 13), and although we did not attend synagogue each Sabbath Saturday, would not allow us to write or cut paper. In stricter Jewish homes (as was with some of my relatives such as the Nusenblatts) on the Sabbath you were not permitted to start any kind of "fire" which ruled out turning on lights, driving a car, or even watching TV. My mom was merciful in that she didn't abide by the fire rule and kept our sacred Saturday morning cartoons alive and well. In this way, she would pick and choose among the many Jewish rules and regulations what we as a family could live with and tuned out the ones that would have been pure torture.

But as for remaining "tribal," while my parents would certainly associate with non-Jews, their deep friendships remained among Jews. They belonged to a Jewish "couples club" and restricted nearly 100% of our social gatherings to friends and families that were also Jewish. As I began dating, my mother kept a keen eye on making sure the girls in my life were also Jewish especially after a cousin or two of mine had actually been disowned by the family after marrying outside the religion (although over the years that eventually changed).

The character of my Jewish experience was certainly not unlike many other cultures in America be they Asian, Greek, Italian, Polish, African American, Irish and so forth in that we pretty much remained and preferred to "be among our own." More importantly, our concern was immediate family first, relatives second, and then Jews in general. Everyone else it seemed was in a world outside of our own.

The Jews (again like many other cultures) were devoted more to the preservation of their culture rather than the welfare of those outside. On the one hand while culture is a treasure of the human experience, it also can lead to a certain kind of isolationism. It's not that we don't *want* to care about another human being regardless of their background. It's just that it's difficult to find much of a reason why we should and perhaps that's the problem.

In a sense we shouldn't *have* to care about anyone. Think about someone that comes to mind that you easily care deeply about like your parents, your spouse, and especially your children. Did anyone need to teach you to care about them? What about some of your closest friends?

The theory I offer is this: *the degree to which we care about others is directly affected by how much in them we can see of ourselves.* That is to say, how much of *you* is part of *them* and vice versa and what we see in ourselves determines how wide the world of caring becomes.

But why should we care to begin with? What benefit is there in caring about others? Here again the problem is not about whether or not we *should* care and any reward has little to do with any benefit derived from caring. Rather caring is the natural result of realization.

There is no ulterior motive to caring about your children. You didn't have to think about it. You cared about them before they were even born. If you see a pregnant woman walking down the street, your "level" of care for that child is insignificant compared to the mother's. But if it is your child then you have become one with that reality. You've realized a connection that requires no effort and is not connected to any benefit. Your level of caring is intense because that child is immediately a part of you physically, mentally, and spiritually. You are essentially dependent upon each other, both child and parent. One cannot exist without the other.

But the origin of whom we are, where we are, and where we are going is not limited to our friends and family. It is connected to an environment far vaster than the small worlds we might wish to protect. Furthermore, perhaps the greatest cause of human suffering (both yours and mine), is that humanity as a whole does not see it this way. But going back to the child/parent example, there is little doubt that the actions of one will not affect the other. Nothing can exist isolated unto itself. One thing always depends on another. Karma/destiny is interwoven with everything. After all, yours is hardly the only bouncing ball in the room. This realization however still doesn't happen simply by grasping its common sense. It actually begins and ends with the process of tapping into that tenth world.

The affectionate "curse" of that world however is the realization of the principle of *dependent origination*. You realize that the process of this happiness cannot continue and develop secluded from this reality because it *becomes* your reality. Furthermore it actually becomes the source of even deeper happiness since you have become more aware of your own humanity.

Caring about the welfare of others then becomes a need for your own personal growth and happiness. They become one but not one... two but not two. Christians may also claim that when one serves God by helping other people, you are reserving your own place in heaven and therefore accomplishing both unselfish and self servicing ends. However, the difference is that Christianity is about serving an outer force and obtaining a theoretical outcome; act and reward are both separate. But for a Buddhist, both act and reward are derived from resulting inner human spiritual evolvement often referred to as *human revolution*.

I'm not ashamed to say that I was at odds with caring for those not closely related either naturally, culturally, or by friendship. But while I have spent some time pondering some historical and cultural connections to Judaism, don't be mistaken into thinking I'm suggesting Christians or anyone else for that matter to be any better. While the premise of Christianity may hold a more universal approach to "all God's children" rather than the "chosen ones," I believe the vast majority of our American society and the world in general easily fits into the first sentence of this paragraph regardless of faiths and cultures and not because they want to be that way.   Contrary, I believe *all* human beings inherently know the common sense and truth about dependent origination but instead have been ingrained by generations of isolationism in which religion has played little if any role as a remedy.

There was a point for me when I became aware of the necessity of accomplishing my goals in balance with living an altruistic existence. In many ways, NSA and even standing out on the street trying to introduce others to chanting was a chance to "fake it until I made it" so to speak. Because of my attraction to Christy, I was led to my first Buddhist meeting and again through May, I found myself willing to explore a new and necessary phase of my own human journey. It was actually my mundane desires that put me in these very positive situations where I was able to continue my own growth: desire at work leading to enlightenment.

Consciousness as Creator

The age old philosophical riddle argued by philosophers for centuries states: "If a tree falls in a forest and there is no one around to hear it, does it make a sound?"

The relevance to this riddle is the issue of human consciousness. My opinion is that nothing exists outside of human consciousness. Human consciousness gives existence to all things. Dinosaurs did not exist until we discovered their now extinct existence. Had we never discovered them, they would have never existed. Forget for a moment whether or not they really *did* exist. Think once again about human consciousness. It's not a matter of the physical. Forget that for a moment. It's a matter of human consciousness. The fact that you are now reading this and perhaps deciding if you agree is proof of my point. For you to even say it is "not true" is to say that it "is" because without you saying or thinking it, it was never said nor was any thought ever given to it. Therefore in a certain way it would not exist.

"Truly, it is more difficult to be born as a human being than it is to lower a thread from the heavens and pass it through the eye of a needle at the bottom of the sea..." [7]

Imagine someone with brain damage and just enough to keep their organs functioning with the help of modern medicine. They are on feeding tubes and any other apparatus that allows their body to continue as a living organism. Blood still flows, lungs still take in oxygen through breathing machines, etc., etc. Everything is black. There is no dreaming, there is no memory... there is nothing. Do they still exist? Well of course they do. Why? It's because you said so and only because you know so. But does that person exist any longer for themselves? I certainly don't think so.

The "creator" (spell it with a capital "C" if you like)... is human consciousness. By *our* very existence

---

[7] The Writings of Nichiren Daishonin, Vol. I, page 125
(Conversation Between a Sage and an Unenlightened Man)

as human beings, we put into existence the environment around us.   Our very own planet Earth is just an organism in a coma without the element of human consciousness.

Let me take that a step further. You can break down the Earth into its many different parts with its' millions of different living creatures, land masses, oceans, winds, its' flowing rivers, molten core, and an eco-system where all things serve a function and depend on one another. You can take a human body and break it down pretty much the same way.   There are also millions of micro organisms, flowing veins, breathing lungs, and all of our organs etc. which are once again all dependent upon one another. You can in fact draw many similarities between Earth and the human body right down to the fact that the human body is composed of about 70% water and the Earth is also covered with about 70% water. It's pretty amazing stuff.

As I just said a moment ago that if you take humans off the planet you essentially have a body in a coma that no longer exists. And there you have it. We have a brain and so does the Earth. It's us! It's all of us. Human beings comprise what can be considered a single brain that makes the planet Earth a living, creative, existing organism.

Now comes the important part.   Your mental health and how it affects *you* is NO DIFFERENT from how the mental health of the planet affects *it*.   Each human being is a living cell of a single brain and one which has gone somewhat insane. You are NOT alone but rather one cell... healthy or unhealthy that contributes to or takes away from the health of this organ... the brain... the consciousness of the planet. It would be ludicrous to think that a lot of unhealthy cells in your own brain would have no affect on this organ and entire body as a whole. Even one step further, the entire universe depends on consciousness for its existence. For without human consciousness life will no longer express itself and ceases to exist.

"Deep in the Snow Mountains lives a bird called the cold-suffering bird that, tortured by the numbing cold, cries that it will build a nest in the morning. Yet when day breaks, it sleeps away the hours in the warm light of the morning sun without building its nest. So it continues to cry vainly throughout its life. The same is true of human beings. When they fall into hell and gasp in its flames, they long to be reborn as humans and vow to put everything else aside and serve the three treasures in order to gain enlightenment in their next life. But even on the rare occasions when they happen to be reborn in human form, the winds of fame and profit blow violently..." [8]

It is through my Buddhist practice that I've been able to go beyond just the simple and perhaps more challenging ideal of "caring" about the welfare of another person or "loving" someone whom I have no past relationship with like that one person on the street so to speak or the neighbor living three houses down

---

[8] The Writings of Nichiren Daishonin Vol. I, page 1027 (Letter to Niike)

from me whom I've never met or a person completely on the other side of the planet. It's about the reality of our existence dependent on one another to become happy. It *is* about happiness. And in the truest sense of the word, our own true happiness cannot be set apart unto itself. The happiness of others, the consciousness of the whole and the causes we make in working towards that end becomes happiness itself. There is no other creature on the planet other than a human being who is capable of this capacity and no other creature that has this responsibility. Yes. Not only *can* you become happy, it is your *responsibility* to become so otherwise you have wasted your own human existence.

Chapter 7

Choices: A Love Story

About two years before the NBC union strike and my return to NSA, I attended a wedding of a good friend of mine who was also a fellow engineer there. Betsy was one of the most strikingly beautiful women I had ever met. With the looks of a young Sophia Loren, her appearance was so intense that she probably scared most men away as a woman untouchable save only for men of great stature to be worthy. But as we became close friends while working together at the NBC Radio Network (as fellow studio engineers) I came to know her as a woman who was perhaps quite apparent of her physical beauty, but unaffected by it. Betsy treasured above all her own dream of family. What a wonderful childhood she must have experienced to have been so grounded in these values. I would even go so far as to say that to her, the physical attributes she possessed where both a blessing and a curse that stood in the way of men seeing her true brilliance as a caring and loving human being who perhaps wanted more than anything else a good husband and perhaps a few, if not many children. And so the day she wished for came true. Betsy was in love and now a bride marrying a struggling musician with a day job. But she seemed happy which was all that mattered.

And so it was at this auspicious occasion that I also would begin a relationship that would become one of the most intense romantic experiences of my life. Her name was Britney. Blonde, petite, and pretty, Britney was a talented young art director working her way up the ladder of success at a major advertising firm in New York. The reception that Saturday became merely backdrop to the immediate chemistry that became obvious to all of our friends. She accepted an invitation to take a motorcycle ride with me the next day and along with Jimmy and his wife we would spend that Sunday together.

From that day on Britney and I would be together at every opportunity. Up to that point in my life, no relationship had made me feel so complete and so vulnerable at the same time. I had never felt so alive.

Both of us were very much in love, dating for almost 18 months and now over 30 years of age, I felt it was time to move the relationship to the next level and ask Britney to marry me. I felt completely ready.

So there we were one night sitting at a restaurant somewhere in mid-town Manhattan excited about the proposal I was about to reveal. But she looked as shocked about the proposal as I was the response, "I don't know," she said. *You don't know?* I was stunned, more so perhaps because I felt something from Britney that went deeper than just uncertainty. It felt more like fear. I was not prepared. I didn't get it.

After making the proposal, the relationship quickly put us in two different worlds. There was no going back to what we were. I had laid all my cards on the table, and they were all hearts while hers were spades. I felt compelled to end it. And so only after a few weeks I found myself standing one night at the entrance of her Manhattan apartment building on 62nd St. and 2nd Ave. gut wrenchingly ending what to me felt like the love affair of the ages. I fought back tears all the way to the subway station and the ride back to Queens. But the events over the next few months in Britney's life would reveal something acutely wrong and the gut feeling of that decision awfully correct.

No more than two months had passed when I was sitting in one of the NBC studios keeping Betsy company while she was editing some tapes. The subject of Britney came up as I discussed how difficult it was for me to get over her. I had assumed it was the same for Britney as well.

"Michael, I guess you didn't hear," said Betsy.

"Hear what?" I asked as I braced myself for the news that she had moved, or goodness forbid that she was in some kind of an accident. Betsy was hesitating.

"Hear *what?*" I again pleaded.

"Britney just got engaged to be married."

The room started spinning. I couldn't have heard that correctly. But it was true. I was overwhelmed.

~~~

There are three typical problems and losses humans go through: health problems, financial problems, and problems involving human relations. I had been through the first two; nearly on my death bed and at times so financially broke without knowing where my next dollar would come from. But nothing can be more devastating than the anguish that can occur from the relationships we have with other human beings or loss thereof. While not making light of serious financial or health problems, you can always figure a way out of a money crunch and even if a disease kills you, there are ways to lift your spirit even until the last moment. But ask a wife who's been abandoned by her husband for a younger woman. Ask a parent who has lost a child. Ask a teenage boy or even a 30 something year old who has just broken up with the love of his life. Nothing prepares you for the broken heart or the unexpected loss of a loved one whether by death or other reasons of separation.

~~~

But Britney getting married? It was only two months ago that she said no to me after an incredible relationship lasting over a year and a half. It felt I had just died a merciless death.

I played old voice mails from Britney on my answering machine several times when I got home; the ones that had meant so much to me. I listened and then I erased as I began to bury any memory of her. But I couldn't erase it from my mind and even became fixated with discovering who could have won her heart so easily and so quickly when for so long it had been mine.

His name was also Michael. He owned a bagel shop on 3rd Ave. north of 63rd Street just around the corner from where Britney was living. I wanted to see him. I had to know who this guy was. With a heavy broken heart and shattered ego I attempted on at least one occasion to go into the store and see who the "other" Michael was. But I never saw him and just continued to chant for the strength to move on.

And move on I did. A couple of months later, I found myself in a relationship to a centerfold quality, 5 foot 9 inch blonde named Michelle, around 12 years younger than me and who I met in (of all places) Disney World, Orlando when my NBC Radio Network program took the show on the road there for a week. It just so happened she lived about 50 miles from New York City in New Jersey. So I was stylin' and pretty much forgot about Britney until one day when I received a phone call.

One night when I got home from New Jersey after visiting Michelle, there was a voice mail on my answering machine from Britney. The immediate sound of her voice sent my heart racing. She sounded desperate while choking back tears.

"Michael, hi it's me, Britney. I'm scared and I really need to talk to you. I was hoping you were there. I'm calling from a payphone outside his apartment. I thought he was going to get violent. Please call me when you can. I just needed to hear your voice. Bye."

She ended up in an abusive relationship? What the hell! And now she's calling me? And why? Did she wake up?

I got in touch with her the next day and later got together for dinner. I told her about Michelle and that I was quite happy although seeing Britney again confused me. I still loved her. But I wasn't willing to consider leaving Michelle and even more importantly knew I needed to avoid Britney's potential double rebound. Nevertheless, Britney and I went to bed that evening and I truly regretted it as it only made things more confusing for me. But there was no joy in having made love to her. Not because of the infidelity to my girlfriend Michelle, but because I was so sad that I was still so much in love with a woman I couldn't be with and for the affection with her that would simply end again in one night. We both knew that we couldn't be together. I made no effort to try nor did she. However, it would not be the last time Britney would enter my life.

Malevolence and Redemption: An Evil Brew

Looking back on my past, there are many choices I could have and should have made that might fall in line with things that I felt I should have done either because of moral values or because I knew they might be destructive in one way or another. We are bombarded from a young age with what is right and what is wrong. Much of this comes from religions we grow up with but there are many general laws in place that are suppose to deter us from committing such acts. It's always a battle of temptation versus consequence and more often than not, temptation often wins. We sometimes move without thinking or maybe even choose not to think before we move.

The law of cause and effect is certainly common among all religions and not a concept owned or invented by Buddhism. I would say however that it is more central to Buddhist thinking than with most other religions particularly when you consider the theory of karma which states that your destiny in the three existences of past, present, and future are all created solely by you and no one else. We have no one to blame but ourselves for "bad" karma. As such we need look no further than ourselves in creating "good" karma.

Karma and the moving karmic balls is nothing other than cause and effect. Buddhism rarely refers to "sin" except in the context of evil acts but not nearly in the same way as Christianity which in some cases teaches the concept of original sin. The idea of original sin has softened in some Christian dominions over the years but like anything else, a concept taught for centuries is hard to shake. Sin, original or not, carries along with it the burden of guilt.

For ages the human being has been at odds with himself in trying to find a balance with morality, ethics, guilt, sin, and the feeling of self despair and self contempt. So heavy are these issues, religions offered a means by which one could expunge their past through various virtuous acts that would offer redemption from sin and evil acts. Most religions offer ways in which one can attempt to shed their sin and their guilt and in the end seek forgiveness ultimately from God. The problematic question I ask is when does God stop forgiving? Is there any point? Do you have a certain quota that you can't exceed? Are there any particular things that you could do that would be just unacceptable and unforgivable? The answer I keep running into from observations and inquiries is simply no. No act is unforgivable no matter how heinous. In the end, it becomes a matter of what one does after the act to find redemption with God. Since all of us are sinners, you seem to have only two choices; a sinner redeemed or a sinner doomed to hell. There are different takes on this, some more extreme than others. But in the end, I don't think it would be mistaken to say that what you do and whom you are judged by becomes a matter between you and "God."

Again, while various degrees of weight are placed on what one does, who God is, and how God redeems (like the various religious spins that provide a human being with his eternal need to find solace in an afterlife), without redemption man once again walks the path of self destruction. If you can't redeem what you have done and are cursed forever, then why not just let it all hang out? On the other hand, if you can be redeemed for anything, then why not just do it with the knowledge (even subconsciously) that you can find atonement for sinning down the road? What a dilemma!

We kill, cheat, steal, use others, and often sanction our government to committing such deeds on our behalf. I don't mean to get political on you but let's face it, besides what we may do as individuals and without being judgmental, consider capital punishment, war, and the acquisition of capital gain and resources all of which may or may not be in what we call our "national interest." What matters is who we are killing, who we are killing for, who we are cheating, who we are cheating for, and who we are stealing from, and who we are stealing for. The "greater good" is always the benchmark of these acts often tainted with shrewdness. We then support either the morality of these acts or once enacted the redemption of any sin caused by these acts through theoretical and literal proof.

Buddhism offers a take on all of this that is quite different and perhaps may explain why Buddhism holds the least violent history of all major world religions.

Think back to our microcosmic analogy of birth and death with sleeping and awaking. You don't get to "fix" your problems with sleep. If you go to bed angry, chances are you are going to still be angry when you wake. If you go to sleep with financial problems, they will not have gone away once you wake up. If you love your wife when you fall asleep, chances are pretty certain you'll still love her when you wake up in the morning. Even suicide becomes an illogical option. You will not escape or change your situation because you take your own life. Like the Emerson, Lake, and Palmer song goes... *"Welcome back my friend to the show that never ends."*

You will not be excused from your causes in your next life. There is no such thing as redemption. In whatever condition you end this life will determine the conditions in your next. You will not be forgiven as there is no one to forgive you except yourself. Furthermore, it is your responsibility to do so. But you must first take into consideration that Buddhism does not dwell on a past that no longer exists. It's gone forever. All that remains is now and the future. This to me is one of the great empowering aspects of Buddhism. *You mean I don't have to feel guilty about what I've done in the past?* To which I ask in return, what would be the point? On the other hand, you can't get away with doing things and getting forgiven for them. There will always be an effect to WHATEVER you say, think, or do. The only past that you are responsible for is the one that brought you to this moment and which you can do nothing about. The only present you are responsible for is the one occurring at this very moment and the only future you are responsible for is the one you are about to create. But once again, we must remind ourselves that destiny is not easily controlled and in a sense an illusion to think we can. However, what we *can* do is "un-trap" ourselves from our own karma.

The law of cause and effect is the only rule that applies to my life. Becoming the "master of my own mind" is a big part of what this journey is all about and one which I continue to challenge. Don't waste time on shame. Regret is the fearful result of a future less lived; a waste of time and energy spent on the consequences of an irresolvable past.

And There She Was

As was often her ritual on her way home from dance class on this warm August evening in 1987, Cristina would often stop at a deli on the corner of 10th Avenue and 49th Street just around the corner of her Manhattan studio apartment to pick up a coconut Frozen Fruit Bar. As she was leaving, bag over her shoulder ready to proceed for a relaxing evening alone, a young woman around the age of 12 stepped in front of her blocking her way.

"Hi, have you ever heard of *Nam-myoho-renge-kyo*?"

Marci was too cute to ignore.

"What?" Cristina replied with her strikingly pretty smile.

Suddenly another young woman ran over. It was Sara, the 19 year old daughter of Roger the attorney who so vigorously ran the NSA chapter that I had connected myself to.

"Hi, my name is Sara!" she said with chipper delight. "What's your name?"

Though uncomfortable, Cristina was too kind hearted to be mean or rude to these two young women who certainly seemed completely unthreatening.

"Cristina," she replied, holding the yet to be opened Frozen Fruit Bar.

"That's great," said Sara. "We're having a Buddhist meeting right around the corner and wanted to invite you to hear about this great practice. It will only take about ten minutes," Sara said nearly pleading.

"Well" Cristina replied trying to keep her smile. "I don't think so, I just came from dance class, I'm kinda' sweated up and I just bought this Frozen Fruit Bar."

At which point Marci jumped in. "You're a dancer? That's great because we are having it at Spence DeCastro's apartment right around the corner and she's a professional Broadway dancer!"

"Well," Cristina said looking for another excuse, "I just bought this Frozen Fruit Bar and it's gonna' melt."

"You can put it in Spence's freezer!" Sara chimes back.

I had arrived back at Spence's apartment after having driven a couple of new "recruits" to our community center near Union Square by 14th Street in lower midtown Manhattan to receive their own *Gohonzon* from a Nichiren Shoshu priest. Not too many New Yorkers owned cars and I just so happened to have inherited my grandfather's 10 year old Buick LeSabre (that had only 10,000 miles on it at the time) after he had passed away a year earlier. Still on strike and trying to support wherever I could, I often volunteered my services and vehicle to shuttle new potential Buddhists *to be* back and forth between the meeting places and the community center. After all, my union was about 2 months into their strike at NBC and I had little else to do except stand on a picket line a few times each week in front of 30 Rockefeller Plaza.

The meeting was already in progress with Roger giving an explanation about the meaning and significance of *Nam-myoho-renge-kyo* and the *Gohonzon*. Along with several members sitting on the floor listening sat Cristina and another woman they had brought in off the street. Cristina looked up and smiled at me as I moved into the room where Roger was standing and talking in his usual invigorated manner. I tried to ignore the attraction.

As she sat there smiling up at me from her crossed legged seat on the floor, I was caught by her pure and humble beauty. As pretty as she was, brunette and petite, she was strikingly authentic in her charm and probably unaware of her own aura that magnetized everyone towards her.

Once the meeting ended and typical of their character, Cristina and another woman were immediately encouraged to get their own *Gohonzon* and begin practicing immediately. Though their wishes to see more people begin their own journey towards happiness were sincere, it was always a bit of a high pressured sales job.

"Oh," said Roger to Cristina, "Why not begin right away?"

"I don't think so," she replied, "I just wanted to hear about this but…"

"You live right across the street," said Sara jumping in and almost up and down like a kid pleading for a new toy, "and Michael will drive you there and bring you back," she said looking over at me.

"Sure," I said with a bit of an uneasy smile.

"So come on," Sara continued.

"It will change your life," said Roger. "And like Sara said, Michael is willing to drive you down there just on 14th Street and I promise you, you will not be sorry. What do you say?" as he stared at her with a frozen smile.

Cristina looked at me and I could almost tell she was tortured by her desire to go home or just appease these people and go along with it to just get it over with. I recalled the feeling at my own first meeting.

"OK," she said. "But this won't take long right?"

"No" said Roger, Sara, and Marci nearly in unison.

"Geez, I can't believe I'm doing this," Cristina laughed.

"Oh it will be great," said Sara joyfully clapping her hands softly together.

"Well..., I don't know... OK," replied Cristina uncertain and nervous.

I don't remember much about the ride down there except that the other woman was apparently homeless and had a bit of a rancid odor. Furthermore, I think someone at the meeting gave her the $15.00 donation fee to the temple required to receive the *Gohonzon*. Yes, it had gone up $10.00 since I had received my own.

As with many other nights in NSA's traditional August and February introductory campaign's, the room was filled with people waiting to receive their own scroll as a Nichiren Shoshu priest and several NSA leaders presided over the ceremony (one of several they held each of these evenings.) I would have to say that most of these people like Cristina hadn't the foggiest idea of what they were doing there as most all of them would fail to follow through with actually continuing any sort of Buddhist practice. It was not for lack of compassion that the NSA members were motivated to get people to begin practicing Buddhism, but the number of *Gohonzons* distributed was definitely outweighing the individuals. A few people would successfully continue practicing but the vast majority would not.

In Cristina's case, once she had received her own *Gohonzon* she began getting constant calls from Sara encouraging her to come to one meeting or another, but was resisting any real commitment as I did when I had first been introduced. But Sara was persistent and used any means to try to get her to a Buddhist activity including using me as bait. Apparently Cristina had asked on one occasion if I was going to be at a particular meeting. I can picture the phone conversation:

"I don't know Sara, I have things I have to do."

"It's really going to be a great meeting and I don't mind coming by and going with you," Sara would enthusiastically reply.

"Well I don't know," then a pause and a giggle, "Is Michael going to be there?"

"Ummmmm yeah, I think so!"

"Well, OK then."

And so while I was actually not at the meeting, it definitely became Sara's new tactic.

Sarah called yet again for another activity, this time the showing of a film about Buddhism.

"I don't think so, I really just got home and I'm tired. It's a movie about Buddhism?" Cristina asked.

"Yeah it's called "The Human Revolution" and we are showing it at a high school not too far away from where you live. I can stop by and pick you up!"

"Nah, I don't think so really."

"But Michael is going to be there," Sara replied happily.

"Oh, alright well maybe."

At the time I was still dating Michelle (the blonde bomb shell from Jersey) and although she was not practicing Buddhism herself she was very supportive of my own practice. And so on the day of the screening, she agreed to escort me. Of course Cristina came as well but unpleasantly surprised to see me with my girlfriend.

~~~

As November approached, it appeared that the negotiations between my union and NBC were finally coming to an end. After six long months on the picket line, we finally settled. However during that time, the division I had worked at for nearly seven years (NBC Radio Network) and the show (Talknet) I worked on for over six years was sold to a company called Westwood One. But since my union was considered a "one shop" union, seniority was not divided up among the different departments of NBC which included their entire New York television department both local and national. As it would happen, many of us working in radio had quite a bit more seniority than those in television and NBC was required to absorb us anywhere they needed to.

All of us were split up into skill training courses within television. Some of us were selected to become camera persons, some maintenance, some audio, and some in television graphics which is where I somehow ended up for my first couple of weeks back on the job. I was chosen to train on a piece of equipment known as Chyron. It's the character graphics generator that among other things puts text on the screen like sports scores, or weather forecasts, or simply the name of a person who is talking on the screen like a reporter or someone being interviewed. Although I knew very little about television technology, I was pretty computer savvy and actually breezed through the two week course. Once that was completed I ended up getting assigned to sit and train with the existing Chyron operator of NBC's TODAY SHOW. My best friend Jimmy also got placed on the TODAY SHOW, but was assigned to be an audio assistant.

Unlike the cozy schedule in radio, the TODAY SHOW hours were brutal. With the show airing each morning at 7:00 AM until 9:00 AM, I had to report to work around 2:00 AM and work either until the show was done or until we completed any post production. Happily however, since there was already a Chyron operator assigned to the show, I was basically just getting in real on-air training and preparing myself to cover when the regular guy would go on vacation. Otherwise I was moving around from one show to another covering for different people but never getting a real gig of my own.

~~~

Sara's use of me from that point became ineffective. Cristina was not willing to come to any further meetings no matter how much Sara pleaded and eventually stopped calling. But at the very least, she was still receiving the organization publication known as the World Tribune and at least had them sitting around her apartment even though her *Gohonzon* was no longer enshrined. But like me when I had first received my own *Gohonzon*, she was at a real crossroad and dilemma with her own future. She began reading self-help books and tried to turn more towards Christianity to help her figure out what she was going to do. Her whole reason for coming to New York was when she was hired by a modern dance company. But not long after arriving, the dance company shut down for lack of funds thanks in part to the Reagan administration's funding cuts for the arts. Working at clerical jobs and still attending dance classes, Cristina was truly at odds with being able to stay in New York as a professional dancer and even considering the very discouraging idea of moving back home with her mother in Daytona Beach, FL.

At some point in February of 1988, she became so distraught without any real solutions to her situation that she began to consider giving Buddhism a shot. She began reading the World Tribunes that contained encouraging testimonials from other members. Finally and on her own volition, she decided to give it a real try.

You can imagine the elation from Sara when out of the blue Cristina contacted her after several months and told her she wanted to know when there would be a meeting. She also wanted to get her *Gohonzon* up again but didn't want to hang it up as before in a cardboard shirt box nailed to the wall. So she decided to take a trip from her 49th Street apartment on Saturday afternoon to the NSA community center at Union Square and 14th Street to see if they might have something at their bookstore that she could use for that purpose.

They were selling an inexpensive *butsudan* made out of cardboard used for enshrining the *Gohonzon* and often purchased by new members just getting started. Cristina, not certain she would figure out how to put this thing together, thought that it would probably be best to attempt it before leaving the community center. At least if she got confused as to what tabs to put into what slots and what parts to punch out and where to fold etc. etc, then at least there might be someone there that would be able to help. That someone would turn out to be me.

For reasons I can't recall, I stopped by the community center myself on that Saturday afternoon. Walking into the upstairs hallway to get a drink from the fountain, there she was. In a pair of black leggings and a denim top, Cristina was fiddling with this box trying to make it all come together.

"Cristina?" I asked with a pleasant surprise.

"Oh! Hey!" as she was also quite shocked.

"What are you doing?" I asked.

"Geez, I can't figure this thing out. Do you know how these things go together?" she asked frustrated and exhausted.

"Sure, let me help you," after having put together quite a few of them for other new members.

"I want to get my *Gohonzon* put up right away and so I figured I would come down here and buy something a little more proper than a shirt box."

"Great," I replied. "Is Sara or anyone coming over to help you?"

"No I just want to get it done, so just figured I would do it on my own."

"Well, I'll tell you what. It's Saturday, I have my car… why don't we just drive up to your place, I'll help you put this together and enshrine it for you."

"Really?" she very excitedly asked. "That would be great!"

And so as it turned out, not only would I escort Cristina back to her apartment to help her re-enshrine her *Gohonzon* but we would also begin dating. It just so happened, that two weeks prior to running into Cristina, I had ended my relationship with Michelle frustrated by what seemed to be problems stemming from the gap in our age (her being 12 years younger than me). And while perhaps that may not matter for say a person 43 years old and one 31 years old, it did when the difference was between someone 33 and the other 21. At least that was my experience.

So Cristina began practicing and participating in NSA activities as we also began dating. It was a good relationship though not necessarily one that was really going anywhere. It was nice having each other's company and friendship. Good conversation was always one of the most important aspects of any relationship. Cristina and I never had any problems finding things to talk about. Between my Jackson Heights, Queens apartment (which had just turned into a co-op and that I ended up purchasing) and Cristina's 49th Street Manhattan studio apartment, we would talk on the phone for hours.

Some time in April and after only having dating for about six weeks, Cristina decided to take a trip down to Daytona Beach, FL for a week to visit her mother and asked me if I wouldn't mind driving her to the airport in Newark, NJ.

On the way there she made a comment to me that would end up goofing with my mind, "Well, at least you'll save money while I'm gone."

Not that Cristina meant anything mean or harmful in what she said, but for some reason after she departed, her comment began to grade on me. Actually I'm sure she meant it with harmless humor. But for whatever reason it turned into a huge turnoff for me. Maybe it had something to do with my relationship to my mother. My mother had a penchant for saying harmless things that somehow ended up being a little inappropriate and which she would realize right afterwards.

~~~

I'll never forget the story my mom told me when right after I had left for New York, she ran into Cindy's father at a large local general store in Mayfield called

Uncle Bills strolling around with their shopping carts. Cindy was the young woman whom I had met in my Jewish youth group during high school, who was going to school in Kansas and who I visited via motorcycle just before leaving Cleveland never to return. Although I hurt Cindy's feelings, I ended the relationship because it was just too difficult with the distance between us while she was in Kansas and me in New York City.

"How have you been?" my mother asked her father.

"Fine and you?"

"Great, just great. My son Michael is in New York now and working for ABC."

"Yes, right, that's great and how's he doing?" he asked my mom.

"Oh, he's doing fine, just fine. And how is Cindy?"

"Well she's still in school at Kansas State, doing well there," her father replied continuing with. "Yeah, it's too bad about Cindy and Michael."

To which my beloved Jewish mother replied and without thinking, "Yeah, that's my son, love 'm and leave 'm!"

My poor mom probably turned 20 shades of red after realizing what had just come out of her mouth.

~~~

So when Cristina had said that to me, I can't tell if had anything to do with some Freudian thing with my mom, but it really bothered me to the point that when she got back home from Florida I told her I felt things were moving too quickly and perhaps should cool it for a while. I was a pure fool.

Cristina was no doubt hurt and confused and I take no pride in saying she was not the first woman that I had hurt because of my own confused ego. But it seemed I was easily capable of becoming defensive and ending a relationship quickly if something felt even a bit wrong particularly having gone through my relationship with Marcia some five years earlier.

But with the support of other members and concern that because of me Cristina might stop practicing Buddhism, she was able to not let this deter her from continuing. I felt bad but right or wrong, I was not willing to allow this relationship to get any deeper and in the end hurt even worse.

About one month later, probably in April or May of 1988, I received a new phone call from Britney once again. I had not heard from her in over nine months and at the time she was apparently in fear of abuse from her fiancé whom she was no longer with. She was just calling to say hello and see if perhaps we could meet for drink or something. I am not going to deny how happy I was to hear her voice again along with the prospect of seeing her. Maybe this time we could make things right. Maybe she went through whatever issues she needed to resolve and was now ready for a new phase in our relationship.

I could tell when meeting her that she was troubled and confused. I could also tell that she missed me and needed me in her life but I couldn't tell how. During our relationship I openly practiced Buddhism although I had still not returned to any involvement with NSA yet. I certainly made no efforts to try to get her to even chant with me. This time however, if any possible relationship was going to begin again, I needed Britney to start getting her own act together and for the first time got her to attend some meetings and begin chanting herself. Around two weeks later, she received her own *Gohonzon*. This was a dream come true for me. Britney was back in my life and while we still did not have any firm commitment to one another, at the very least she was now sharing in this practice and I still could not deny my desire to have her back in my life.

Fearful of asking her again to marry me, I decided to at least try testing the waters for both of us. I had a ring that was given to me by my grandfather when I was a little boy that while it could no longer fit any of my fingers, I always kept it safely tucked away.

"Listen," I said to her at dinner one night. "I still very much want to consider spending my life with you but I'm not going to ask. Instead, I was wondering if you would take this ring as sort of a pre-engagement with no commitments. You don't have to put it on, or you can put it on occasionally to see how it feels. And if the time comes, then it comes."

"Oh Michael," she said with tears in her eyes. "I will do that," as she kissed me. I thought that life was not only good, but better than ever.

Suddenly and for no apparent reason, Britney disappeared not long after that night. I was baffled. These were the days before cell phones so while I left messages on her apartment answering machine and messages for her at work, she stopped returning my calls. In the meantime however, I was not going to let myself get dragged down with this anymore. After all that had happened with Britney, then Michelle, then Britney again, then Michelle again, then Cristina, and then Britney once more, I had enough. For the first time in my life women no longer mattered to me. I just didn't care. Probably a good thing for me and a better thing for the entire female population of New York City! I had new challenges from my work at NBC and while I had missed several large NSA conventions simply because I was inactive for one reason or another, a July 4th, 1988 convention was planned to be held in Worcester, MA with a parade and events at a large sports arena in the city. In spite of that however and before knowing about the convention, I had promised my mom (who with my dad had moved to Orange County, CA six years earlier), that I would fly to California and attend my cousin Kirk's wedding in July but which was also happening on the same exact day as the convention. So I began to at least try and support the other members as best as I could in spite of disappointingly not being able to attend the event. I opted in favor of not taking a chance in disappointing my family.

At NBC, what I thought was an opportunity for advancement and recognition of a job well done on Chyron, I was asked if I would like to begin working in full graphics for the TODAY SHOW. The room that provided graphics for the show like animations and various other effects was like mission control; dark and dimly illuminated only by the hundreds of lit buttons all over the room. Even for someone in the industry like me it was overwhelming. It was filled with TV monitors, a large Grass Valley television control switcher, an Abacus still picture storage and playback device, just to mention a few of the major devices including its own Chyron (the ONLY piece of equipment I was trained on and really knew).

I jumped at the opportunity! Considering the two weeks of intensive and dedicated training that NBC provided me for just Chyron alone, I anticipated that there would be even that much more training. But to my incredible dismay and confusion, I was informed that there would be no training! Instead I was told that I would have to learn simply by watching the current graphics engineer and only had a few weeks to figure it all out.

Not only was the engineer annoyed with having been put in that position (whose attitude I could easily sense), we had to begin pre-production at 12:00 midnight! I was no doubt placed in a position to fail by the management of NBC who after the strike had more employees than they really needed, a union to contend with, and a strike that had just ended some 8 months prior. If they couldn't fire you, they figured out a way to fail you out.

They basically gave me two weeks to pull this off. With no real grasp of even television technology itself, I was asked to absorb all this information on a graveyard shift when the mind is fighting the need to sleep let alone forcing it to learn from the regular engineer who made me feel unwelcome each night. I can't actually blame her for feeling that way as I had quite a bit more seniority than her. She may have been dealing with the thought that she was training a person who could take her job away.

So as all this was going on in June of 1988, NSA was embarking on an intense push toward the Worcester convention that was a little less than a month away. While I knew I could not attend, I wanted to assist in any way possible. This included supporting rehearsals for a men's steel drum band which was going to perform both in the parade and in the large city sports arena.

Almost each weekday I would get back to my apartment around 10:00 AM from having worked through an entire night of stressful concocted training, get myself to try and sleep with the sun blaring in, wake up just before it would turn dark again, eat something, and then head back into the city by subway to participate in some meeting at someone's Manhattan apartment, and then head back to 30 Rockefeller Plaza to once again begin working at midnight. I was so tired and exhausted, I recall being the first member to arrive at a meeting one evening. I sat down on a couch in the back of the room facing the *Gohonzon* and began chanting. Suddenly the room was filled with people chanting whom I never saw come in. I had actually passed out where I sat while chanting.

With only a couple weeks left to go before the convention in Worcester, something had come over me. I didn't know why at the time, but I was compelled to reconsider the choice of attending my cousin's wedding in California or support my friends in New York and attend the Worcester NSA event. I knew that my family would be upset with me, in particular my mom and sisters. In spite of practicing this Buddhist *thing* at that time for nearly 13 years it was still not something they would understand but I was willing to take the heat. So while I would have to miss the wedding, I changed my flight reservations in order to fly out and visit my parents on the day following both the wedding and the convention. And as I expected, I got a *why are you doing this* call from my sister Debbie in California after having disappointed my mom by telling her I would have to miss the wedding. I had no way of explaining this to either my mom or sister. I simply said I just had to make this choice and couldn't illuminate the rationale to them let alone even to myself for the sudden decision. I'm sure my cousin would forgive me as we were not all that close, but events like weddings and bar mitzvahs were used as opportunities to bring the entire family together (as best we could) with all of our aunts, uncles, and cousins.

Buses from New York and other cities such as Boston and Washington DC, arrived in Worcester, MA as thousands of Buddhists from NSA emerged on the city to participate in a large parade with various performing groups after which we would hold a large NSA convention meeting. The master of ceremony that day was Patrick Duffy, a long time Buddhist and member himself, famous for his staring role in the famous 70's television series *Dallas*. So there I was with about 20 other smiling men in pastel shirts and white pants in what was known as the NSA Men's Division Steel Drum Band about to take our place in the parade along with a slew of marching bands, dance groups, and floats. It was a beautiful July 4th as we proceeded to march and play while Caribbean dancers followed behind.

As each group ended its march along the mile long route, we all entered the large sports arena and took our designated seats. Sitting with my comrades of the Men's Division Steel Drum Band we listened, watched, and played along with NSA performing groups from various districts around the east coast. Included in the festivities was an NSA brass band, a fife and drum corps band, a taiko drum band, a seven story human pyramid on roller skates put on by the NSA Young Men's Gymnastic team, a performance by Suzanne Vega (a member herself just coming off her 1987 hit single "Luka"), and a number of speeches that included several testimonial experiences.

One performance in particular caught my eye. It was from the NSA Young Women's New York Drill Dance Team. As they locked arms spinning around in unison, there was one particular person that I suddenly became mesmerized with. It was Cristina. It was like the "dance at the gym" scene in West Side Story when Maria walks into Tony's sight. When their eyes meet the attraction is so intense that the world around goes into a blur. In their minds they begin a dance with each other. Of course the only dance happening for real was the one Cristina was doing on the arena floor and the only dance in anyone's head was the one in my own unbeknownst to her.

I obviously knew Cristina. I had dated her briefly and broke up with her because of my own insecurities. But now I saw something that was not anything my mind could comprehend. I was no longer seeing just a woman, or just a person. I was seeing something far more. I was peering into my future and the partner I needed in my life.

Even as the NSA General Director George Williams delivered his speech to the large near capacity crowd, I don't think I even heard a word of it. Something was happening to me. It became crystal clear why I had needed to make the choice of being at the convention. It also was more proof of how my dedicated struggles towards my Buddhist practice was paying off and how it was bringing out and affecting this "wisdom" or Buddhahood that we've been talking about.

~~~

We hear many stories from people all over the world regarding how they have heard a "voice," sometimes associating it with a message from an outside source like God and in turn act upon it. Regardless of where that voice is coming from, the question I ask is when do you know it's a "message" that you must follow or something that you simply want to hear and therefore hear? In the end, perhaps only time can tell if you actually "followed the voice of wisdom" whether you want to call it God or call it your own.

~~~

Although I was in the stands while she was seated on the floor of the arena and probably a good 50 yards or more away, I somehow was able to catch her attention. I had to talk to her. I gave her a "finger phone" signal indicating that I needed to talk to her. And although she looked incredibly confused, she nodded.

Sitting on the bus going back home, I couldn't explain how incredible I felt and how excited I was to get back to New York. There were clear changes I needed to make and found the courage to make them. Besides what I was feeling about Cristina, it also became clear to me that I needed to get out of NBC. I made a decision to resign once I returned from vacation. Since having sold my co-op and with money in the bank, I had to take a chance and go after my dream no matter the cost or how long it might take. There would be no better time than immediately. I had graduated from film school and had always desired to complete a screenplay. I just needed to take the chance. There was no thinking about it.

As soon as the buses arrived I started calling Cristina's apartment whose bus apparently arrived quite a bit earlier since we had more to do before leaving Worcester.

"What's up?" she asked.

"I need to see you," I said.

"Right now? It's getting little late don't you think?"

"Cristina, listen. I have to talk to you. It won't take long I promise. I can be there in 20 minutes."

"OK," she said hesitantly after a pause.

It was probably already near 10:00 PM and I had to get ready to fly out to California the next day. Instead of taking a chance on getting a subway, I immediately jumped into a taxi and headed to her West 49th Street apartment.

After climbing the stairs to her unit I gently knocked on the door.

"Michael is that you?"

"Yeah, it's me."

"Hold on," as she began unbolting the locks.

As she opened the door I could tell it was rather dark and she had already had her sofa bed pulled out and had gotten into bed.

"What's up with you?" she asked.

"Listen, do you mind if I come in for just a little bit," I asked sincerely. "It's really important."

"OK, but I don't know what's so important this late. It's been a long day."

"I know," I said as I entered and closed the door behind me realizing that she was most definitely annoyed.

She lay back down in her bed and pulled the covers up. "I'm really tired," she said with a slight chuckle.

I sat down on the other side of the bed with my back to her and then twisted myself around without saying anything. None of my feelings had changed and it felt so real and so incredible. I could tell by the look on her face that she was getting a little impatient with me. "So?" she asked.

"So," I repeated. "I… love you."

"Huh?" she asked thinking perhaps she had not heard correctly.

"I love you." I repeated but this time showing more confidence.

"Huh? Are you crazy?" she asked.

"Maybe, I don't know. Something strange happened to me at the convention. When I looked at you, and saw you there… I don't know. I realized that I was in love with you."

"Geez," was her reaction with a half laugh. "Oh man, I can't believe you came all the way over here. What time is it anyway?" she said looking over at her alarm clock. "Almost eleven o'clock. Oh my God. Are you nuts?"

"No, I'm not nuts. I love you," and with that I laid my head down on the pillow next to her.

"Oh my God. This is insane," she said, but at least she was smiling. She placed her gentle hand on my face, "You've got to be crazy."

"I'm not." I then kissed her as she kissed me back.

"This is insane!" as though she were thinking this might be a dream; and not necessarily a good one.

"Yeah, I know."

I was certainly hoping that it wasn't just because she was exhausted from the entire day's activities that she was allowing me to say all this without kicking me out.

After a short period of time and knowing it was getting late I just kissed her and said goodbye.

"We can talk about this in a week when you get back from California," she said as I was about to leave.

And with that, I left her apartment headed back to a New Jersey condo I was temporarily staying at with a friend.

The very next morning I headed to Newark Airport to catch my flight. Sleep had not "brought me to my senses." I knew that what I was feeling about Cristina was deep and correct and was more than certain this was the woman I needed to be with.

As I stood there in the airport with nearly an hour left before having to board my plane I suddenly became consumed with a crazy compulsive idea. I was about to leave for a week after having come to one of the most important realizations of my entire life. I called Cristina from a pay phone.

"Hey, it's me."

"Hi! What's going on?" she asked.

"I'm at the airport waiting for my flight."

"What time does it leave?"

"Hey listen," ignoring her question. "How would you like to come to California with me and meet my family?"

"What?"

"I'm going to buy you a ticket for tomorrow and leave it here at the airport. Will you do it?"

"I... I don't know," she replied with some shock and hesitation.

"Come on, you don't have anything better to do, right? I'll call you and give you the details once I have the ticket."

"Can I think about it?" she asked.

"Yes you can, but I'm buying it anyway. It will be here. Use it if you want and call me to let me know if you are coming."

As told to me by Cristina, she started calling around for advice. One of her closest (non-Buddhist) friends reminded her that I was the "jerk" who broke up with her six months earlier and advised her not to go. She then called Diana a mutual friend, actress and fellow Buddhist who asked, "Have you ever *been* to California?"

To which Cristina replied, "No."

"Then what the hell. You get on that plane girl!"

A little more than one month later, I asked Cristina to marry me and she accepted.

Chapter 8

Move Over Move Over, Let Wisdom Take Over

B ack in the mid-seventies when I first tried sushi, the thought of eating uncooked fish was quite detestable (as it was for most Americans). Today there are dozens of sushi restaurants all over the United States and in most major cities. There is even one on Mayfield Road right across the street from where I attended elementary school! Hell, people didn't even know what a taco was where I was growing up when the only Mexican food around could be found in my mom's kitchen.

Of course our minds are malleable organs that can be "forced" into doing things it may not want to do. The idea of "acquiring a taste" in something like food, wine, music, and art is a prime example of forcing our minds to try something it is telling us that it's not going to like. Sushi caught on as a social fad and many Americans pushed themselves into giving it a try, perhaps more than a few times before the taste caught on.

If you're a sushi lover like me, at one time you may have assumed that you would never like it. The thought of eating meat from an animal that was not cooked didn't seem all that appetizing. But you took control. Your mind failed in its attempt to keep you away from sushi because another part of you wanted to experience the craze. A little peer pressure perhaps.

None of us like going to the doctor especially if it's going to be painful. But we are willing to subject ourselves to the ordeal because the consequences of not going might be far worse. Filing taxes is not particularly thrilling but certainly a better alternative than going to jail. Reading text books, studying and doing homework can be agonizing but the consequences of failure are far more detrimental. Choosing an apple over French fries may not be as blissful but it helps make our image in the mirror a little softer on the eyes.

If you are a parent, you already know the frustration you feel when you can't prevent your child from making some of the same mistakes you made. But in the end, we realize that many of those experiences are what helped us grow up and become responsible citizens in society. Painful experiences are an unavoidable necessity of leading happy and productive lives. Like it or not, no pain, no gain.

While the examples can go on and on, we are all aware that the road to fulfilling our desires also involves unpleasant choices. Painful experiences can also have much needed benefit in moving our lives forward.

We can challenge our minds' refusal to try something new as well as forcing it to take on activities that we consider an anathema. We may also have to fight its addictions to things like over-eating, wrong relationships, and time wasted on couches. It's a mind that sometimes is at a loss for control in its effort to consume stimuli that it believes will give us happiness when in the end it often leads us to miserable outcomes. And so once again, who really *is* in control?

Wants and needs, needs and wants. I want this but I don't need it. I need this but I don't want it. I need to not want it. I need to want it. I want to need it. I need to do this but I want to do that. I want it because I need it.

Can somebody please tell me what I _need_ *for goodness sake?*

Not only do we want to be happy, as humans we need happiness as it is our fourth basic desire. But we need to get back to the crucial question; *what is it that I need because what I want (or what my mind says it wants) just can't be trusted.*

Number 9, Number 9, Number 9

Many people think that the moral of the *Wizard of Oz* is that "there's no place like home," as Dorothy proclaims in the final line of the film. But I see the moral of the story being contained in the glass slippers. The Good Witch explains to Dorothy that her ability to get back home had always been in her power. This to me was the great message. If getting "back home" could represent absolute happiness, then Buddhism proclaims that you've always had the power within to get there but were never made aware of it; powers beyond your imagination. The power I refer to goes beyond the power of positive thinking whether you want to think it's some sort of secret or not. Remember, we are talking about happiness that goes far beyond whether we simply solve our financial, weight, or relationship problems.

Long before modern psychology, Buddhism talked about nine levels of consciousness:

#'s 1 through #6 includes our five senses plus conscious thought.

#7 is the well known "sub-conscious" mind where modern psychology does most of its digging.

#8 is the storage of the "bouncing balls." In other words, that's where all your *karma* is stored; past, present, and future.

And finally #9 is where pure consciousness resides unaffected by any other level of consciousness and where you can find your glass slippers.

Perhaps a clearer way to describe the 9th level is that it is the purity of everything. What makes you... you. Forget your personality and your likes and dislikes for a moment. What is the essence of who you are; who you are as a human being? What makes a rose a rose, a fish a fish, and a human a human?

Take an iceberg. An iceberg is made of water and floats in an ocean. In order to describe these levels, let's consider that the first 7 levels from all of our five senses all the way down to our Freudian sub-consciousness are but the tip of the iceberg peeking out from the top of the water. The 8th level where all of your karma (or destiny) is stored is the gigantic body of the iceberg below. And finally, the 9th level of consciousness is the water itself that includes the entire vast ocean. The only way to get to the 8th level is by tapping into the essence of the iceberg itself; water.

Tapping In

Talent is an inherent benefit in someone's life that makes them potentially extraordinary in one thing or another. But even if you have the talent to become the greatest mathematician of all time, it doesn't just happen. While it may even be true that this talent can be recognized at even an early age, it takes hard work and many years to bring that talent to its greatest potential. *Potential* is the key word here. No talent however great it may be can come to fruition unless the person possessing the talent is presented with the right circumstances. So long as the right conditions are present, the person must often go through a tremendous amount of challenges and periods of internal growth and understanding before this talent can really come forth.

Because of our superior brains, we human beings possess certain inherent potentials that other living creature's do not. Furthermore, while other animals may be able to adapt to certain environmental situations, we are the only species that actually "advance."

I recall an argument I once had with Britney who was a strict vegetarian. A popular diet book published in the mid-80's supported the notion of a vegetarian diet as the natural way that humans should eat. In helping to make its case, the book pointed out how blunt and rounded human teeth are more naturally like animals that are plant eaters rather than carnivores. At the time it seemed to make really good sense. In fact, I couldn't really find a reasonable argument (although I wasn't prepared to give up meat).

But eventually it dawned on me that because of our superior intelligence, our bodily characteristics have very little to do with what we can or cannot eat. Man's ability to harness fire solved that problem by allowing us to cook our meats and make them tender enough to chew with our measly human teeth (not to mention the invention of knives and forks). In fact, we've outdone just about every animal on the planet with talents that only they at one time possessed. We can fly higher and faster than any bird although we were never born with wings. We go to ocean depths far deeper and move through water much faster than any creature in the sea. We can move across land and terrains with far greater speeds than the fastest moving four legged animal. Human beings can be birds, fish, jaguars, and yes, even carnivores. While I'm not trying to make a case one way or another on what would be a healthier diet, what I am saying is that nature didn't make human beings vegetarians because of our teeth anymore than it didn't give us wings to fly or gills that allow us to swim under water. The rules of physical attributions or limitations do not apply to the human species.

So what does all this have to do with *happiness*?

While we have advanced from the invention of the wheel to space stations, internal true happiness which involves insight into life and death is the one discovery that seems to elude us. But like the inherent talents we possess as individuals and as a species, this is also something we have always possessed. If we view internal happiness in the same way as an inherent talent, then we must also realize that in order to develop and bring it out, we must work at it. The talent we inherently possessed that took us to the moon existed thousands of years before we ever got there. It just took a little bit of time to work it all out. The process of human beings discovering the way in which to bring out their own inner state of happiness, confidence, and courage is in no way different. We as a species are still working towards getting there.

The Three Evolutions of Mankind

Another great difference between the human mind and that of other creatures on the planet is that we were cursed with the need for *reason*. The dictionary definition of *reason* I'm referring to is *the mental powers concerned with forming conclusions, judgments, or inferences.* No other species on the planet has this mental power other than us humans.

When we speak of evolution, we normally refer to the physical evolution of our species. However, there are two other forms of evolution which are just as significant and which both derived from reason; scientific evolution and spiritual evolution. Reason on the one hand is one of mankind's greatest gifts because it compels him to explore while on the other hand a great curse because it forces him to cope with that which is incomprehensible.

We know how ridiculous it would be today to reconsider the world to be flat. For centuries mankind also believed in a multitude of gods to explain all the aspects of the universe he couldn't understand. Eventually we evolved into a one God concept and from there to a "loving" God where we were suppose to be compelled not only with our own salvation but with that of others. Herein lay the history of Western religion.

And when you really think about it, all this stuff has really taken a very short period of time. I'm guessing, but let's say ten to fifteen thousand years from when mankind began actually recording history in one way or another. Ten to fifteen thousand years… that's it! Consider the possibility that if we don't destroy ourselves, we should hopefully exist maybe another one or two *billion* years. If that becomes the case, we have not even existed .0008% of a 2 billion year existence. We *should* have a VERY long way to go!

We have quickly taken for granted the many mysteries that have been uncovered by our scientific discoveries. But science too has its limitations as even Albert Einstein concluded and that only religion can hope to resolve.[9] We may no longer view our planet in the center of the universe but the vast universe within which we call *life* is still the one great mystery. The true reason behind human suffering cannot be scientifically cured. As time moves forward and even as science rapidly advances, we begin realizing that humanity cannot invent, fight, drug, positively think, or politicize itself out of endless suffering and potential annihilation. Nor can it be solved by suppressing our desires or by simply following a set of rules. There are no political, scientific, or military solutions that can ever bring about a peace in the world that man still has yet to experience in spite of all his religions. In America while we have lived in somewhat of a sheltered world, it continues to weaken because of our dependence on foreign energy sources, terrorism, the wars that have resulted, and from

---

[9] *"The religion of the future will be a cosmic religion. It should transcend personal God and avoid dogma and theology. Covering both the natural and the spiritual, it should be based on a religious sense arising from the experience of all things natural and spiritual as a meaningful unity. Buddhism answers this description. If there is any religion that could cope with modern scientific needs it would be Buddhism".* **(Albert Einstein, source unknown)**

an economy that no longer relies solely on productive American labor.

As the cold war developed in the 50's and 60's, we began associating more and more our constitutional right to pursue happiness with that of Capitalism. In a sense while economic systems in theory, the battle took on the characteristics of a religious war; Capitalism vs. Communism. Happiness and our right to it became more and more associated with what we owned and how much money we could earn. Freedom became synonymous with a person's inalienable right to raise their stature in society as high as one could reach. It seemed as though even our religions themselves embraced the ideal of a God given right to prosperity. Communism was therefore not just a differing of economic opinion. It actually took on the traits of anti-Christian sentiment. Communists were portrayed as messengers of Satan himself. Not only did God give us permission to be Capitalists, we were encouraged to live the life of an anti-Communist. American society merged religion with an economic system that became an apparition of good vs. evil. Does this sound familiar with the world today? It was propelled even further and gave rise to the "me" (and perhaps most decadent) 80's with the fall of the Soviet Union as a victory proving once and for all that Communism was a failed system while Capitalism prevailed. And while we can make the argument that the Soviet Union was never really the true Communism that Marx had envisioned, we must ask ourselves the question, *"OK we won the Cold War. Now what exactly did we win?"*

It's no wonder that many of us have grown more cynical of religion as it continues to prove its penchant knack to cause more anger and divisiveness rather than the love and sanctity for life that their teachings proclaim. In short, America has become a society at odds with itself. Can science, politics, or even the power of positive thinking replace religion as a solution to happiness? I don't think so. Rather, we will eventually begin realizing that the answer to our problems as a world will need to come from the continued development of our inner spiritual evolution.

A New Kind of Faith

Faith in Buddhism is based on experience. Seeing *is* believing as opposed to *believing* is *seeing*. A western religion like Christianity requires one to profess belief first. In fact no on enters the fold without *first* believing (accepting Jesus Christ as your savior for example). However, there were no pre-requisites asked of me when I began chanting except that I chant. I didn't even understand what I was doing. I didn't understand the translations of the words that I was reciting and in particular the main phrase itself, *Nam-myoho-renge-kyo*. I believed in nothing and was never asked to believe in anything.

To draw upon an over-used analogy in Buddhist circles, if I didn't believe that an elevator would get me to my floor, I see no reason why I would get in. But I was a child when I first experienced an elevator and had very little idea what I was getting into. My faith was based solely on the experience I had with my parents and thus was able to completely place my trust and faith in *them through my experience*, not in the elevator. Of course after having ridden elevators hundreds of times since that first experience, I certainly don't think twice about getting into one nor do I need my parents to be with me when I enter. My faith in elevators is based upon continuous actual proof. I was never asked to believe in elevators. I'm sure most of us rarely contemplate the process of getting into this little box that takes our precious lives and thrusts it hundreds of feet from the ground in a matter of seconds.

Unless we can see concrete proof that chanting has validity, then there is very little point in continuing. This concept is often very different compared to other religions and how our material desires become fused with our spiritual growth. The process of believing and understanding happens gradually. But whether you believe in or understand the mechanics of that elevator you get into, chances are pretty certain you're going to get to your floor (positive results perpetuated from previous positive experiences). This is Buddhist faith. In fact Buddhism considers "actual" proof the most important of what are called the "three proofs"; theoretical, literal, and actual.

We are also capable of denying ourselves any gratification particularly when it comes to proof of religion. Theoretical and literal proof can often be enough; but why? Many religions are largely reliant upon predictions, prophecy, and conjecture (all based on scripture or literal proof) that help support theoretical proof most particularly theories of what is in store for believers in the afterlife. But as humanity continues to evolve (along with scientific evolution), theoretical and literal proof become less and less sustainable. Buddhism is not nearly concerned about these other two proofs and most concerned about actual proof. Furthermore, it should be theoretical and literal proof that supports actual proof, not the other way around. I find it a distinct difference between Buddhism and most other religions. But also bear in mind that the law of causality was not invented, discovered, or is owned by Buddhism. Anyone regardless of any religious affiliation can gain "actual proof" of this law by the good causes one makes despite whatever label they may attach to it.

Lest we forget however, the primary point of Buddhism is not about getting things. It's about becoming a human being and achieving our fullest potential AS A HUMAN BEING which involves more of an internal realization rather than external gratification. On the other hand, without external gratification, there is no life. For example, you can't live without food. So gratifying your body with nutrition is essential. If on the other hand you could not gratify your hunger no matter how much you ate, either you would kill yourself by becoming 1000 pounds or starve yourself to death because eating would be useless. The entire universe works in this manner. Gratification becomes part of the symbiotic relationship we have with our environment. It is a principle of life.

Since wisdom is not a process controlled through our conscious minds like the decision making process that is derived from our thoughts and five senses, we must rely upon our experiences to continue Buddhist practice. As a Buddhist, tapping into the "water" of my wisdom or that inner eye that guides me to what I *need* to become happy, relies completely on one thing and one thing only; my choice to continue chanting. That's it. And of course it would be pretty difficult to keep chanting unless I was getting proof it was all worth the effort.

Buddhism therefore is based upon the principle that desires can transform themselves into enlightenment and one cannot happen without the other. You cannot deny your desires and yet they can destroy you. But you cannot sustain this journey unless you have proof that your desires are being fulfilled. Otherwise Buddhism would be reduced to nothing more than blind faith.

Reviewing once again, the first and foremost purpose of the 3 basic desires of food, shelter and sex is survival of the species. But as humans these "basics" are also enhanced by our fourth human desire; the need to find happiness. We also know that when left to their own devices, our pleasure seeking minds can easily get us into trouble. Like many other things, religions pounded us with the evil and destructiveness of desire. Break down the Ten Commandments for example and you'll find it's all about squelching desires rather than embracing them:

	Commandment	Which squelches...
1	No other gods or idols.	...any desire to explore new expressions of spirituality.
2	No using God's name in vain.	...any desire to blame God for anything.
3	Keeping the Sabbath.	...any desire to forget about the tedium of religion all together.
4	Honoring your parents.	...any desire not to live by our parents' wishes and commands especially when it comes to religious beliefs.
5	No killing of another human.	...any desire to kill another which is the ultimate destructive expression of anger.
6	No adultery.	...any desire for sex that may potentially destroy families. But in addition, religious groups have used this commandment to condemn any sex outside of marriage thereby trying to squelch non-marital sex all together.
7	No stealing.	...any desire to get something that doesn't rightfully belong to you but rather someone else.
8	No bearing false witness.	...any desire to lie.
9	No coveting thy neighbor's wife, house, ox, slaves, etc.	...any desire to envy the possession and successes of others. More importantly, not viewing possessions as God's decision and a diminution of His will

		(regardless of what you have or what someone else has).
10		Depending on which version you look at either # 1 or #9 are split in two making for 10.

The common sense of many of these commandments is unarguable but it's not the moral point that I'm looking at here.

For thousands of years, religion has prosecuted desire as the basis for evil and self destruction. Well then, I think we probably should add an eleventh commandment to keep up with the times. It was probably a little too early to explain to Moses mankind's eventual temptation of such future delights as Twinkies and Burger King after he had climbed up Mount Sinai to receive the commandments. So here goes: *"Neither shall you place within, that which does not provide what is necessary to sustain the body of God's great gift of life."* Add that and from number five on down you would be pretty complete in keeping in check all destructive desires that could annihilate life, allow for unfettered sexual engagement, social discord from the taking of others, and then add number eleven and you get to the more modern destructive desires of over-eating, drugs, and smoking. The first few commandments (including number 4) serve no purpose other than the preservation of the belief system itself which without those probably would make 5 thru 10 (and my additional 11th commandment) pretty worthless anyway.

So for hundreds and hundreds of years, western religion has made filthy and vile humankind's most basic trait; desire. Original sin began with the taking of the apple in the Garden of Eden and the wickedness of temptation. And yet you look at America which is predominantly Christian-Judaic, read statistics where nearly 90% of all Americans believe in God and have to wonder about the insanity of it all. There is a plethora of killing, a plethora of stealing, and a plethora of lying. Our young people are constantly faced with the growing cynicism of a political structure that is continuously falling apart. Apathy begins leading to non-direction that then leads to misdirection. This is a dilemma. Living in a country whose strong self-declaration of adherence to God and faith finds little if any progression towards a society reflective of those principles. In fact, it appears we are even moving further away from them.

So has modern man moved away from the ability to function as religious automatons, living productively, peacefully, and in cohabitation with his environment simply by following rules? Am I saying that the teachings of western religions are flawed? As to the second question, I'm not knowledgeable enough about the testaments (old and new) or about the Koran to make any such judgments. But frankly from what I do know, in principle they find a lot of common ground in the goodness of what they are suppose to achieve. However, I don't have to be an expert or an authority to proclaim that generally speaking western religion has been extremely ineffective in having much of an affect on the ills facing western society. And while that certainly does NOT mean that there are not good morally well intentioned Jews, Christians, and Muslims who not only talk the talk but walk the walk, I cannot see any progressive social or worldly value being gained by their efforts. Nor is this to say that eastern religion and Buddhism itself has been free from its own historic malaise of futility. It was in fact Nichiren Daishonin's rebellious proclamations about all religions that existed in Japan during his day (which included various forms of Buddhism) that were serving little purpose other than to themselves.

It's a simple question: *why does society continue to worsen when at their core, the founders of all religions were seeking ways to eliminate human suffering?* Is it because the theoretical promise of heavenly afterlife become the only prize left for religions to offer? Certainly it's not one that our youths can rally behind as young people are too young to contemplate death anyway. We can tell by the way they drive. The easy answer might be because there are not enough Christians who have committed to the message of Jesus or enough Jews and Muslims who have committed themselves to peace (or at least that's what I think they might tell you).

The issue comes down to what I would call the *Conundrum of the Relevance and Reality.* What religions are relevant to humanity in the 21st Century and what is the reality of their effects on society at large? In America, there is often a separation between what we do in our religious lives and what we do to generate material gain. Sometimes they are actually in conflict with one another. Morals derived from religion clashes with morals (or lack thereof) surrounding what a person may or may not need to do in order to gain something in their own personal life (be it financial, relationships, or any other material element). It's not necessarily a matter of whether religions have *adopted* to modern society, it's more a matter of where conflict lies at a fundamental level.

This Buddhism has never had any interference with desire. Furthermore we use desire not only to find proof but more importantly to move us towards enlightenment. Compare this to other religions that carry behind them doctrines that promote such things as abstinence (not just sexually but in all material matters), relinquishment, and self denial as dignified manners of living. It is not a matter of whether desires will end up controlling you, but in the end if you can transform and control them in a positive direction.

Chapter 9

Object at the Center

The Ring

While we had gone out and purchased an engagement ring, I also wanted Cristina to have the ring that my grandfather had given me and the one that I had asked Britney to hold on to. But even though several months had passed, Britney would still not return my calls. I was at a loss as to what I could do.

So certain were we about our future together, Cristina and I saw no point in a long engagement. I proposed on August 9, 1988 and we set a date for October 29th of the same year. I was so thrilled about the fact that we were not even going to live with each other but instead our lives would come together for the first time as husband and wife. Of course, that's more like the golden olden days of our parents. Now it seems more the norm to live together before making the big marriage move.

Well aware that I had resigned from my position at NBC before accepting my proposal for marriage, Cristina was willing to face any challenge with me. This made it even more evident that she was the woman I was looking for in my life. It's difficult to face the battles in your life with a partner who cannot welcome the challenges as his or her own. More importantly, I stand in awe of the capacity of a woman's heart. OK, well certainly Cristina's heart. But women constantly meet challenges that would crumble even the most stouthearted of men.

One of my great prides of being associated with Nichiren Buddhism is the consideration and attitude towards women and the equality of human beings in general. It's easy to berate history in regards to how the world has treated women and the indistinguishable preciousness of all human beings regardless of gender, race, sexual orientation, or social stature. What's most extraordinary is how a man in the deeply seated inequitable culture of 13th century Japan was able through his own enlightenment realize the correctness of all human equality.

~~~

In his quest to become the "wisest man in all of Japan" as he promised at age 12, Nichiren's discovery was not met with kindness. Quite the contrary, he had to constantly fight for his survival having been attacked, exiled, and nearly killed on several occasions. It was not only through his own single-minded compassion for the Japanese people and humanity at large, but the incredible dedication of many of his disciples who valiantly supported him even at the risk of their own lives. In fact three farmers were beheaded for refusing to give up their faith under government pressure. Realizing that others would be willing to sacrifice even their own lives, the incident famously known as the Atsuhara Persecution, was pivotal in Nichiren's decision to inscribe the *Dai-Gohonzon* for the benefit of future generations.

As he continued the establishment of his teachings, he wrote hundreds of personal letters of encouragement to various followers, edification of his teachings, and treatises all of which were ardently compiled after his death in what is known as *Gosho*. (Painstakingly translated into many languages around the world, the English version is titled The Writings of Nichiren Daishonin Volumes I and II.)

Unlike the founders of just about all the major world religions including Judaism, Christianity, and Islam, Nichiren Buddhism holds the great treasure of having the ability to reference and study his actual writings rather than relying on ancient hearsay and interpretation of what the true intent of the founder really was. Whether Buddhist scholars are in agreement or not, Nichiren was not seeking to create just a new interpretation and sect of Gautama's (Shakayamuni) teaching. Rather he was departing from what he felt Buddhism *was* to what Buddhism is *meant* to be for modern man in the period predicted by Shakayamuni as the third and final period of Buddhism known as *mappo*[10].   Nichiren Buddhists do not in any way consider Shakayamuni as their teacher or mentor, but rather Nichiren himself.   Perhaps the best way to describe the seriousness of this departure is to compare it to Christianity's departure from Judaism.   Nichiren Buddhism finds it roots in Shakyamuni's teachings but again only in the way Christianity might find its connections to the Old Testament.   You will not find any images of any Buddha's either in the form of statues or drawings in this Buddhism.

The attacks on his life and his teachings came swiftly once those in authority began fearing loss of power.   Not unlike many other examples throughout history when established religions or governments feel that they may lose their power to control common people and culture, the attacks were relentless and lasted from the time Nichiren declared his discovery at the age of 32 until he died at the age of 61 in 1282. He declared that enlightenment was not reserved for any particular class, status, or gender of people and could be shared by all. Here are a few quotes that illustrate this example:

---

[10] Shakayamuni had predicted three periods of Buddhism. The first two being 1,000 years each after his death and the third and final period being for 1,000 years and until eternity. The period known as *shoho* was when Shakayamuni's teachings would benefit human beings, the second known as *zoho* when his teachings would lose their power to benefit and finally *mappo* or the period when the *Law* would be revealed as described in the *Lotus Sutra*. Nichiren had determined that he was living about 200 years into this final period known as *mappo*.

"Only in the Lotus Sutra do we read that a woman who embraces this sutra not only excels all other women, but also surpasses all men."[11]

"...but more than laymen or laywomen, it is the priests with perverse wisdom and hearts who are the Buddha's worst enemies." [12]

"...whether priests or lay believers, whether eminent or humble, all can hope to attain Buddhahood."[13]

In the dark night and early morning of September 12, 1271 Nichiren was arrested and taken to a beach in an area known as Tatsunokuchi by samurai soldiers for the purpose of execution. Accompanying him in fervent protest, one of his staunchest and most devout followers, a samurai named Shijo Kingo, swore that he would also die along his side. But they held Kingo back as they proceeded to drag his mentor in position for beheading. As Nichiren chanted *Nam-myoho-renge-kyo* a samurai took his sword and raised it above Nichiren's head while Kingo continued to scream towards his mentor his pledge to follow him even to death. But just before the soldier was about to sweep down his fatal blow, a comet or some sort of orb lit up

---

[11] The Writings of Nichiren Daishonin, Vol. I page 464 (The Unity of Husband and Wife)
[12] The Writings of Nichiren Daishonin, Vol. I page 1028 (Letter to Niike)
[13] The Writings of Nichiren Daishonin, Vol. I page 873 (Those Initially Aspiring to The Way)

the night sky. The samurai soldiers were startled and immediately began to run fearing an omen and devilish curse would befall them.

The picture in my mind is that of Nichiren, after having anticipated his final moment instead was yelling at the fleeing soldiers to return and finish what they had started. I then see Shingo Kingo crying as he begins to untie Nichiren's hands. At this moment, Nichiren was never so certain of his mission or his identity.

"Finally we came to a place that I knew must be the site of my execution. Indeed, the soldiers stopped and began to mill around in excitement. Saemonnojo in tears said, 'These are your last moments!' I replied, 'You don't understand! What greater joy could there be? Don't you remember what you promised?' I had no sooner said this when a brilliant orb as bright as the moon burst forth from the direction of Enoshima, shooting across the sky from southeast to northwest. It was shortly before dawn and still too dark to see anyone's face, but the radiant object clearly illuminated everyone like bright moonlight. The executioner fell on his face, his eyes blinded. The soldiers were filled with panic. Some ran off into the distance, some jumped down from their horses and huddled on the ground, while others crouched in their saddles. I called out, 'Here, why do you shrink from this vile prisoner? Come closer! Come closer!' But no one would approach me. 'What if the dawn should come? You must hurry up and

execute me – once the day breaks, it will be too ugly a job.' I urged them on, but they made no response."[14]

As word spread of the incident, the authorities themselves were at a loss as to how to quell the teachings of a single priest. He was arrested again shortly after and this time exiled to a remote area of an island known as Sado in the hopes that they would never hear from him again as conditions would be so harsh that this would be tantamount to a death sentence. To make things even more difficult, the government made certain that false rumors were spread to the island's inhabitants regarding the arrival of the "criminal" Nichiren so that he would find even more enemies to greet him.

"At last I reached the province of Sado. There, true to the nature of that northern land, I found the wind particularly strong in winter, the snows deep, the clothing thin, and the food scarce."

He then goes on to say, *"My dwelling was a dilapidated grass-roof hut in the midst of a field thick with eulalia and pampas grass where corpses were buried. Rain leaked in and the walls did not keep out the wind. Day and night the only sound reaching my ears was the sighing of the wind by my pillow; each*

---

[14] The Writings of Nichiren Daishonin, Vol. I page 768 (The Actions of the Votary of the Lotus Sutra)

morning the sight that met my eyes was the snow that buried the roads far and near."[15]

Left with little clothing and in a dilapidated structure that was not capable of protecting him from the wind, snow, and freezing cold, Nichiren even then realized in the midst of this environmental hell that he was the happiest person in the entire world.

"I, Nichiren am the richest man in all of present-day Japan."[16]

Freedom is not something that governments grant us. True freedom is when your life is free from the illusions of desire and no longer shackled by the fears of death. True freedom is a true sense of self and clarity of purpose as a human being.

Around 3 years later Nichiren was pardoned from his exile. Even in the direst of conditions he would write some of his most important writings as many of his followers did whatever was necessary to help him survive.

"From Kamakura in Sagami Province to the northern province of Sado is a journey of more than a thousand ri over treacherous mountains and raging seas. There are sudden onslaughts of wind and rain,

---

[15] The Writings of Nichiren Daishonin, Vol. I page 519 (Letter to Horen)
[16] The Writings of Nichiren Daishonin, Vol. I page 268 (The Opening of the Eyes)

bandits lurk in the mountains, and pirates lie in wait on the sea. The people at every stage and every post are as bestial as dogs or tigers, and you must have felt as though you were undergoing the sufferings of the three evil paths in this life. Moreover, we live in troubled times. Since last year rebels have filled our country, and finally, on the eleventh day of the second month of this year, a battle broke out. It is now almost the end of the fifth month, but society has not yet been restored to peace and security. Nevertheless, despite all the risks, you traveled to Sado carrying your infant daughter..."[17]

~~~

Cristina and I continued to prepare for our wedding but at the same time were both participating in as many NSA activities as possible even arriving at the New York NSA Community Center at 6:00 AM each morning to chant.

One cool September evening I had just stepped outside the community center after a meeting I helped lead. Wearing a suit and tie, I walked over to a payphone just outside the building on Union Square and East 14th Street. I wanted to check in with a local meeting being held by one of the groups in the chapter I was responsible for. The apartment where it was being held was just a few city blocks away. Initially I was planning to go straight on over to the Port Authority and catch my bus back to the condo in New Jersey. But they informed me of a couple of guests who were interested in hearing more about Buddhism and asked me if I

---

[17] The Writings of Nichiren Daishonin, Vol. I page 325 (Letter to the Sage Nichimyo)

would be willing to come by and help. I told them that I would rush right over and immediately jumped into a taxi.

The meeting went great as I had a chance to talk with the two individuals who came to their first meeting. It appeared they had a very genuine interest in giving the practice a whirl. Though delighted with the result, I was suddenly hit with a sickening feeling in the pit of my stomach. I realized that a fanny pouch containing my wallet (with quite a bit of cash), and my checkbook was left at the phone booth where I had made the call about an hour earlier before heading over. I quickly left and jumped into another cab heading straight back down to Union Square and that phone booth. What would be the chances after an hour that my stuff would still be there?

As I feared, there was no fanny pouch in sight. I felt a little panic come over me as I realized there were copies of my signature, identification, and a book of blank checks that had a balance in the account of nearly $50,000. It was everything I had. Furthermore there was nothing that would help identify where I could be reached (just in case someone honest may have picked it up) since all my addresses and phone numbers still had the Jackson Heights, Queens; information I had just recently moved from.

Already after 9:00 PM and getting dark, I didn't know what to do. Left with few choices, I headed back up the stairs of the community center to chant. There were very few people left inside as they were beginning to close up for the night. I went into the main Gohonzon room and began chanting feverously. As I chanted,

Jack, a senior in the practice walked through the room. (Jack was Marci's father; the 12 year old girl who first approached Cristina who was holding a coconut Froze Fruit Bar outside a deli one August evening before going to her first meeting. Come to think of it, I don't think Cristina ever went back to Spence's apartment to get it out of her freezer). I immediately grabbed him to get some encouragement and guidance with regards to my situation.

"Well, the first thing you should do is go back out there and look in any surrounding garbage baskets," he said to me. "If some homeless person picked it up they would only be interested in the cash and would throw the rest of it away," he said with a warm and concerning smile.

"OK," as I replied trying to keep my spirit and confidence up.

"But here is what you should really do." His face turned ever serious and he pointed at me. "While you are looking out there you must chant."

"I will," I replied.

"No, you must chant for a great experience. Something you can share with all the members and everyone else. You must somehow make this a great experience. I want you to chant with that attitude!"

Although hard to feel his passion at the time, I agreed to do it.

"Good luck!" he then said with a smile as I walked back down the stairs.

It was now around 9:30 PM and dark outside as I began sifting through different city street garbage baskets around the vicinity while it seemed the only ones left on the streets were the homeless and me. But I chanted none-the-less as a light rain began to fall thinking in my mind that I would have a great experience and would be able to encourage others. I can't remember how many trash cans I looked through, but after about 30 minutes I started giving up hope of finding it; searching trash cans in the rain wearing a suit and tie. What a site I must have been to onlookers including the homeless.

Finally, I called Cristina and gave her the news. She began to cry as all the money we had to start our new life together might be lost if the wrong unscrupulous person were to get a hold of it. New York is certainly one of the largest cities in the entire world. Millions and millions of people go through and work in Manhattan every day. As much as I loved this great city, it is not necessarily a forgiving one.

I assured her that I had just enough money to get myself back home to New Jersey. As best I could, I tried comforting her into thinking that everything would be alright. As I rode home on the bus finally meeting my destination at the New Jersey condo, I contemplated the race against time I would have once I woke up the next day. As soon as the banks opened I would have to put a stop on all of my checks and protect anything else I had.

The rain thankfully had dissipated as I began approaching the front door. Already past 11:00 PM, I heard the phone ringing inside. I quickly ran up fumbling to find the key and fit it into the hole. After unlocking the dead bolt I then had to find the other key to fit into the door knob.   The phone kept ringing. Flinging the door open without shutting it behind me I ran into the middle of the living room where the phone was on top of a desk and quickly picked it up.

"Hello," I asked as I was panting for breath.

"Hello," a female voice with a southern accent replied on the line. "This is Shirley and I'm an MCI operator."

"Yes?"

"Is this Michael Friedman?"

"Yes."

"Sir, did you by chance lose a wallet tonight?"

"Yes!" I nearly screamed into the phone.

"Well I have on the line with me a person named Julie who says she found it. Go ahead ma'am."

Another female voice came on the phone, "Hello?"

"Hey!" I replied excitedly.

"Is this Michael?"

"Yes! Oh my God!" I exclaimed as I held my forehead in my hand in total disbelief.

"I found your whole fanny pack with everything inside of it." I had to sit down almost not being able to believe my own ears as she continued. "I lost my own purse just last week and thankfully the person that found it was honest and contacted me right away. So I felt like I had a debt of gratitude I had to repay. It was not easy to find you."

"How *did* you find me?" I asked.

"It wasn't easy. I checked almost everything but your phone was disconnected even though you were still listed in the directory. Apparently you must have moved. So I found your MCI phone card and called them. I told them what I was trying to do and they cooperated by locating you."

"Wow, I just don't know how to thank you," I said to her.

"Like I said," she replied, "you don't owe me anything. I was simply paying back the favor done to me."

"Well OK," I said feeling all giddy, "How should we do this, can I meet you somewhere tomorrow?"

"Sure, that would work. I can meet you near my office. I work around 56th Street and 6th Avenue," she said.

"Oh I used to work around there. I used to work for NBC at 30 Rock. Who do you work for?"

"I work in advertising. For a company called D'Arcy, DMB&B."

Did I hear her right? "Did you say D'Arcy."

"Yes, are you familiar with it?"

As if the evening were not bizarre enough, my heart began to pound. "Do you by any chance know someone named Britney Pierce?"

"Britney?" she said with a matter of fact attitude. "Sure I know her. She works at the desk right next to me."

I went silent. I could not believe what I was hearing. This woman who so generously used her ingenuity and perseverance to find me in order to return my belongings worked along side Britney; *my* Britney! After a pause she asked, "Why, do you know her?"

There must be at least 8 to 10 MILLION people that live and work in New York City and it just so happens that a person who works alongside *Britney* finds my belongings?

"Hell yes I know her!" as I went on to explain just how.

"This is really bizarre. What do you want me to do?" she asked.

"I want you go to work tomorrow and give my stuff to her. Tell her she needs to call me. I'll get my stuff from her."

"Are you sure?" she asked to confirm. "I can do that."

"Yes, please do that. Let me make sure you have my number."

As I expected, the next morning the phone rang.

"Michael."

"Britney."

"I can't believe what happened this morning. Julie walked up to my desk and shoved a picture ID of you in my face and said to me, 'Do you know this guy?' I thought this was a of set up," she said laughing.

"Why had you never returned my calls?" I asked her.

"I don't know," she replied after a pause and sigh. "I don't know. Just a lot going on in my life. I'm sorry."

"That's OK, forget it," I said. "I obviously need to get my stuff back."

"Sure," she replied.

After a pause I then said, "I would also like to get my ring back that I gave you. The one my grandfather had given me."

"Sure, OK. How about if we meet for a drink or something tonight near my place?"

"OK," I replied. "That would be fine."

Considering that Cristina had been aware of how I had once felt about Britney, I wasn't sure how well she took the news about me meeting Britney for a drink in order to get my stuff. But I suppose looking back, Cristina may have been thinking to herself that I needed to do this and she needed to know where I stood for her own sake.

There Britney sat sitting in the dimly lit garden terrace of a neighborhood restaurant; the woman who at one time meant more to me than anything in the world and whom I offered my entire life to. We hugged and kissed each other on the cheek. As we sat down at the table, she handed me my fanny pouch.

As our drinks arrived and after some catching up conversation, I couldn't help but wonder where the ring was.

"So," I said, "I wanted to get my ring back."

"Yes, of course. I forgot it. It's at my apartment," she said.

I wasn't sure if I could believe that she would have forgotten it but I had not yet told her about Cristina.

"Britney," I said looking into her eyes.   "I'm engaged. I'm getting married."

She just stared at me for a moment, "Wow."

That was all she said. Suddenly she began to cry like I had never seen her cry before.   It was uncontrollable and I didn't know what to do. But she seemed so embarrassed we had to leave the restaurant. I quickly paid for the drinks and had to nearly chase her out. During the entire walk around the corner to her apartment and all the way up the four flights of stairs to her unit, we said nothing as she continued to sob.

She was shaking as she unlocked her door and as I followed her in. She opened up a small box near her bed and from it took the ring and handed it to me.

"I'm sorry Britney," I said to her as I started to leave. "It wasn't like I didn't try."

Hearing the dead bolt lock behind me, I looked back at her door. As much as I had once loved her, I had moved on. Cristina was my life partner and I was never so certain about anything else in my life. I descended the stairs of her building knowing full well I would never again return.

The Gohonzon

It was a beautiful day that October 29th, 1988 as we held our wedding at the Nichiren Shoshu temple in Flushing Meadows, Queens. I stood at the front of the room facing our friends and family as I watched Cristina enter. She was so beautiful as my eyes began to tear with joy. It was a new beginning for my life.

We wouldn't take our honeymoon until February of the following year as we both were very busy helping renovate a marvelous new building that NSA had purchased on 15th Street just East of 5th Avenue and which would become the New York SGI Culture Center. Working day and night, members from all over New York were pitching in to make a critical deadline for its' opening.   There were times that I was so exhausted I would even fall asleep on the floor in some parts of the building wherever I was working.   Helping carpenters lay down base molding, demolishing walls, removing paint, or whatever was needed, this is where Cristina and I spent the first few weeks of our marriage.

One early evening after coming home from working there, I plopped myself down on the couch as Cristina was getting ready to go into Manhattan to attend a meeting.   Since we still had my grandfather's Buick LaSabre I had inherited, it was not really a problem to commute from the Jersey City brownstone we rented although the car itself was starting to show signs of wear from the unforgiving city streets.   As she was getting ready to make it in for a 7:00 PM meeting she walked across the living room.

"Do you want to come with me?" she asked.

"No.   No way!   I just got home and I'm beat.   I can't imagine going back into the city again!" I replied after having worked at the culture center since very early that morning.

"OK, no problem," she said with an easy attitude of complete understanding.   Smiling at me, she gave me a kiss as I lay there and started to walk down the stairs.

Suddenly I shouted out to her, "Honey wait! I'm going."

I was dog tired and didn't have any idea why I said that or what came over me, but suddenly I was walking down the stairs, driving through the Holland Tunnel back into Manhattan and north on 10th Avenue with Cristina at my side.

Not more than about 2 miles up from the tunnel I heard a loud thud-like sound come from under the car. I immediately knew what it was. I had just put new straps on the gas tank which apparently were put on wrong and snapped off dropping the tank filled with gas to the street as the car would continue to drag it. I stopped the car at once and looked underneath confirming my assertion. Not only did it drop but it also ripped a small hole in the tank slowly leaking gas. Within sight and only several blocks away I spotted a gas and service station. I knew that if I could drive the car ever so slowly I could get there safely without creating any heat or sparks which is what I ended up doing.

But what if I had not been with Cristina? She certainly would not have known what that sound was. Would she have stopped immediately or dragged the tank long enough and fast enough to create heat, dangerous sparks, and a potential explosion. What got me to stand up at the last minute to go with her when I could have easily and without remorse stayed at home?

~~~

We *can* see our karmic strings and change our destiny. Remember, we talked about a difference between magic and mystical. There is nothing magic about chanting to this scroll known as the *Gohonzon*.   I have always chanted for anything I wanted without reservation. It doesn't have to be something intangible like pure happiness for example. I wouldn't even know where to begin to chant for something like that. But it's easy to chant for health, more money, a better job, a relationship, or for a friend.   If I was able to get everything I chanted for (in other words if chanting was clearly just conspicuous prayer leading to a conspicuous result), then no doubt this Buddhism would be magic or voodoo.

We had talked about the Ten Worlds in a previous chapter using an example of the gambling obsessive husband who was caught between the worlds of heaven or hell depending on what the environment dealt him. In fact none of the Ten Worlds are capable of coming about on their own. There is always a "trigger" from our environment needed to propel us from one world into another. Furthermore, there is a "method" of communication between the external and the internal. This communication can come through any of our six basic senses of sight, sound, smell, touch, taste or thought.   It is even an illusion to think that we are somehow separate from our environment, for if we were, we could exist in a world void of any such stimulus. In order to exist within the reality of life (*ke*), we are in one of these Ten Worlds 100% of the time, all the time.   It is only in death (*ku*) when all of these worlds go into dormancy until we are born again.

Getting ourselves into the first nine are fairly simple for anyone to understand. However, galvanizing the great prize of the transcendent tenth world is what has baffled and motivated Buddhists for centuries even before Nichiren's time.   While Nichiren rejected all other schools of Buddhist teachings some of which taught that it took an uncountable amount of lifetimes of austere Buddhist practice to reach enlightenment or even the idea of "nothingness" as taught by such schools as Zen, he understood that all human beings could equally attain this state of being (in their present *form*) no matter if you were educated or uneducated or your status in society whether a learned priest, a person of wealth, a peasant, a common man or a woman.   Furthermore, he also understood that like all other worlds, the world of Buddhahood also required communication with the outer world.   It cannot simply come about on its own as with all other nine.

The conclusion was that *Nam-myoho-renge-kyo* was the means by which the tenth world could communicate to the stimulus of the enlightened life condition embodied in the *Gohonzon*.

Every object has within it a mystical bond to someone or something.   Consider the book you are holding right now.   Every page of it has some mystical bond to me and my entire life for without me and the life I've lived, it would never have existed.   Maybe you're wearing a pair of Levi jeans right now.   The existence of those jeans is mystically connected to a man named Levi Strauss who was born in Bavaria in 1829 and everything about his life.   Had he not existed, you would either be wearing some other pants or sitting in your undees.   Every piece of furniture you own, every street you walk on, everything you purchase, everything you eat has deep mystic connection to something other than the "thing" itself. Some things mean more to our lives than other things. Some things are insignificant and of little value. I doubt very much that you contemplate the life of Levi Strauss each time you put your jeans on. Some things on the other hand may even be priceless to you as the connection(s) to it is what gives it value; my grandfather's ring for example. But in the end, what gives them value? Of course we do, but at the same time we don't. The object has inherent value but only if there is means of communication that allows it to express any value.

Take the jeans again. If someone just gave them to you, then perhaps they would be less significant than if you had used your own money to buy them. So now there is a connection between the jeans and the value of the money spent on them. If they look really good on you, then there is further significance in how the jeans have communicated with your sense of outward appearance. If you had nothing better to do, you could become a scholar of Levi Strauss and the industry he created giving them even more significant value because now you have communicated with the object on an entirely different level. But whether or not you knew something or nothing about the jeans, the object still has a mystic connection. So while you may give it more value yourself, you had nothing to do with the value that is part of its inheritance. Take even just a name:

"India comprises seventy states, but they are known collectively by the name India. Japan comprises sixty provinces, but they are known collectively by the name Japan. Within the name India are contained all seventy states, as well as their people, animals, treasures, and so forth. Within the name Japan are contained all sixty six provinces. The feathers sent as tribute from Dewa, the gold of the province of Mutsu, and all the other treasures of the nation, as well as the people and animals, and temples and shrines, are contained within the two characters that form the name Japan."[18]

So even in speech or writing, words have deep mystic meaning. The depth of that word and its value to you will depend upon how you've communicated with that word. The more you know about a country for example, the more the name of that country will mean to you. But even if you had never heard of a country, it wouldn't make it any less and its connection to that country remains as a constant.

So here you have a scroll that contains a bunch of Chinese characters called the *Gohonzon* that to most people means nothing at all since very few of us can read what it says. But like the country you never heard of, does that make it less significant? Because your mind can't translate the words to a literal message does that mean it therefore has any less meaning? You don't know my grandfather since you never met him before he

---

[18] The Writings of Nichiren Daishonin, Vol. I page 732 (On Repaying Debts of Gratitude)

passed away in 1986. You can't read anything about him and therefore the only information you may learn is that which I might share with you. But let me place the ring that he gave me in your hand. Does the ring still have an inherent connection to my grandfather or doesn't it? Even if you picked up the ring laying somewhere on a sidewalk without even knowing whom it belonged to, would that eradicate its connection to my grandfather or me? In a sense, it could be argued that even inanimate objects including words have profound mystical connections that in a sense give them "life." And while they cannot express that life without some connection to something animate, they none-the-less carry that potential.

The *Gohonzon* is the complete expression of Nichiren Daishonin's enlightenment. Or perhaps I can explain it this way:

Suppose that you are a young boy with magnificent baseball potential. Your hero is the famous star of the New York Yankees, Alex Rodriguez. You watch and study him as much as you can. How he swings a bat and how he fields a ball. You watch everything from the pivoting of his hips to his point of release when throwing a runner out at first base. How he thinks when he leads off and how he is able to anticipate the pitcher's movements to make a steal. Arguably the most talented baseball player in the league, you yearn to be as good as Alex. Perhaps you even have the talent potential to be just as good or perhaps even better.

But it's not Alex the man that means anything to you. It's Alex the baseball player and the abilities that he was able to achieve and develop in himself. And if it were possible for Alex to somehow extract this talent into written word that contained everything that defined his passion and ability he might hand it to you and say, "Hey kid, here it is. This is the thing that you so worship about me and the thing which you yearn to become yourself."

Alex can't actually do that, but suppose he could. Suppose he was able to extract even symbolically what represented his talent. You could look at it with the knowledge that you had the same potential and somehow be able to center your life on becoming the same as the "thing" he is. And in a sense, regardless of whether he was able to put it into physical form on a piece of paper, his presence in this life still allows you to center yourself on bringing out this same potential talent.

Since Nichiren knew he would not live any longer than the 61 years he did, he understood that in order to "stimulate" the same enlightened life condition in that of other people, he would need to bring it forth into physical form that would remain forever.

"I, Nichiren, have inscribed my life in sumi ink, so believe in the Gohonzon with your whole heart. The Buddha's will is the Lotus Sutra, but the soul of

Nichiren is nothing other than Nam-myoho-renge-kyo. "[19]

I am told that the word *Gohonzon* literally means "true object of worship." However I would rather refer to it as the "correct object at the center." I say this with no authority other than the one that helps me make more sense of it.

We become products of that which we center our lives on. Those centers will shift and perhaps quite often. But the question is; *what do we truly regard as the most important thing in our life?* For some it may be a sport, or a personal relationship. Maybe it's our careers or our children. Maybe it's our health or our physical looks. Maybe it's our religion, a political ideology, knowledge, or a charitable service of some kind. But as I just mentioned it may be one thing and then another.

What is meant by "true" or as I prefer "correct?" It's not about right or wrong. It's not about this way or no other. It's about what is *essential*. So you may ask, essential for what? Well, you would at least agree that there is a thing called essentialness. For example, there are many factors essential in sustaining life like the sun. It is essential that you eat and drink to live and that you rest and take time to sleep. There are essentials in modern society that we accept as a community like having a job and earning money.

---

[19] The Writings of Nichiren Daishonin, Vol. I page 412 (Reply to Kyo'o)

So now we circle back to *need* versus *want*. Obviously with all of our religions, self help gurus, alleged "secrets", and spiritual/material mixtures, we have yet to find any solution to the constant death, destruction, and overall emptiness that has plagued human beings since recorded time. The reason is simply this: *human beings for the most part have continuously mistaken the ephemeral for the essential.* If we are dependent upon the rhythmical cycle of things like that of our planet circling around the sun, our beating heart, or even the principle that our machines cannot run properly unless they have rhythm like our automobiles; if we know for a fact that without food, clothing, or shelter, or the ability to reproduce that we would perish, then we have accepted the concept of essentialness.

From the point of view regarding absolute happiness, is it essential to have money? It helps. Is it essential to be in love? It certainly feels good. Is it essential be healthy? It certainly beats being sick. Is it essential to see our children do well in school? Well it certainly makes one proud. The answer is that it is not essential for any one of these things for a person's ultimate state of happiness. That's right NOT essential! They are all of the ephemeral.

But what then is essential to trigger the tenth world or this ultimate state of happiness? What is essential is that you can tap into the wisdom that you've always possessed and that is inherent within you. You can't possibly attain this kind of pure indestructible happiness unless you have the confidence that you are "seeing" the strings of your karma. You can't possibly find this happiness unless you can somehow stop making the same mistakes over and over again. You can't possibly find this happiness if you can't make the right choices. You can't possibly find this happiness unless you understand your place in this world. You can't possibly find this happiness unless you can shed certain illusions about what happiness really is. You can't possibly find this happiness unless you can recognize the preciousness of your life and see that in everyone else as well. And perhaps most importantly, you cannot possibly find this happiness unless you can resolve the mystery of life and death; a knowledge that is already within you. The only way that any of this is possible is by centering on your own wisdom. In a sense, it's worshipping the very essence of your own life. Don't mistake this into thinking that I'm suggesting "self indulgent" worship. This goes far beyond your ego and who you are in this life.

Since Nichiren was able to achieve this, he was able to translate it into physical form. In fact inscribed on the *Gohonzon* are all of the Ten Worlds but with *Nam-myoho-renge-kyo* inscribed boldly down the center with Nichiren's signature at the bottom representative of a life that has centered itself on the tenth world; the World of Buddhahood. It is not important if our minds cannot comprehend this. Remember, there is always a mystical connection of any object to its source. Therefore, the *Gohonzon* is an object mystically connected to the enlightenment of Nichiren himself. Since Buddhism is not a process of belief but rather proof of a process, I can only offer you my word to those who do not chant.

Essentially it is through the boy's effort to center himself on Alex Rodriguez's talent that he was able to bring forth the same talent within himself. So it is therefore not Alex's talent that he worshipped, but in the end his own. He only used the talent of Rodriguez to bring it out. We use the enlightened life condition of Nichiren much the same way. Chanting *Nam-myoho-renge-kyo* to this *Gohonzon* is the "method" of communication between what is in us and the object that can stimulate our essential wisdom. It is through this communication and ONLY through this communication that this scroll has any worth. Furthermore, if you were to think of this "object of worship" as something that had some power on its own to do *anything* other than help you bring out your own inherent condition of enlightenment then you would be practicing a different religion and not the Buddhism of Nichiren.

"Never seek this Gohonzon outside yourself. The Gohonzon exists only within the mortal flesh of us ordinary people who embrace the Lotus Sutra and chant Nam-myoho-renge-kyo."[20]

We do not worship Nichiren as a person or anyone else but rather we make the "essential object at the center" his condition of enlightenment so that we can tap into our own wisdom (the essential element) and

---

[20] The Writings of Nichiren Daishonin, Vol. I page 832 (The Real Aspect of the Gohonzon)

eventually bring out the same inherent condition in our own lives.

Vow and Mission: Entering the State of Non-Regression

The World of Buddhahood or Enlightenment is not some kind of everlasting euphoric state. You don't suddenly become unaffected by your problems. It's one of the Ten Worlds like any of the others. It can come and it can just as easily go. But in the process of shifting your "center" or dominant world to that of the tenth as illustrated in the *Gohonzon* (whether you possess one or not incidentally), you begin understanding and taking control of the law of causality. This in turn brings forth a confidence and courage to face head on any of those problems because in the end you are no longer uncertain if you will win or lose. Imagine that.

In over 30 years of practicing this Buddhism I have *never* known anyone who has stuck with this practice and failed in their lives. No one; not a single person. I'm not saying that I haven't seen people facing setbacks. Hell, I've had a few of them myself. But in the process of shifting our dominant world, we begin realizing that our "problems" can themselves become periods of growth and great joy.

The key (as I mentioned earlier) is in continuation.   Whether in Buddhism or any other endeavor, nothing of great value can come from a partially completed journey.

"For example, the journey from Kamakura to Kyoto takes twelve days. If you travel for eleven but stop with only one day remaining, how can you admire the moon over the capital?"[21]

It is a principle of life that all great journeys must first begin with a great vow which is the same as a promise and a great mission that becomes the foundation of that vow. Look at some of the great explorers throughout history like Christopher Columbus who is credited for discovering the Americas, James Cook who chartered the great Pacific Ocean, and Lewis & Clark who in 1803 began the first great journey across what would eventually became the entire continental United States. Were there any points in their undertakings when things looked impossible and where they wanted to quit and give up?

I think of my own life as a great journey. Every human life can and should be viewed in this way. It begins with birth and should end with a final moment when we can look back and have no regrets. For in the end, we take nothing with us except the balance sheet of what we will be leaving behind. And it's not money or fame. Our "immortality" lives on only through a ripple effect brought about by the people we've touched and

---

[21] The Writings of Nichiren Daishonin, Vol. I page 1027 (Letter to Niike)

the lives we've helped profoundly change. One of the greatest moments of my entire life was walking down the streets of New York one evening. Along side me were my friends Jimmy, Elaine, Tim, and Vicki. Looking over at them I realized that because of me, they were able to profoundly change their own lives. I don't think I can remember a more fulfilling moment.

While we may not begin our journey with any promise or vow, in order to sustain the voyage we must at some point make one. We may only begin with the hope that we can find a way to solve our problems and that's perfectly fine. But what do we need to sustain the journey? And not only sustain it, but enjoy it even through the problems we will inevitably face?

At this point I can only speak for myself but hope you will allow me to do so. As I conclude with my confession:

My life is only as great as the promise that I can make to an ideal and my willingness to accomplish that goal. I cannot trust my mind, yet know that once controlled, my mind can give me the passion I need to complete this life's journey without regret. If that means seeking out a mentor from which I can find this vow, then so be it. Whatever it takes, my life and those around me are far too precious to succumb to the illusions of my own ego and not allow my full potential to come forth. I am neither a good person who creates value with my life nor a bad person that denigrates life but simply a person capable of either.

Epilogue

Bringing It Together

I would continue my own challenges and journey over the years that followed my marriage to Cristina in 1988. We would leave New York four years later and move to California not only with the hopes that one of my screenplays had sold but to also be closer to my parents who had moved there from Cleveland ten years earlier.

My first two screenplays were very well received. *"Parkersfield"* the first one I completed, was picked up by The Gersh Agency, one of the entertainment industries premier talent agencies even before the ink was dry. The work was passed around to several producers in Hollywood but never picked up. However, based on a film that came out not long after, I had to wonder if it wasn't stolen. Before leaving New York I then completed my second work, *"Jedburgh"* which once again generated a lot of excitement even enticing a producer to fly into New York from California and spend a day with me going over the story and revisions. But I never followed through. In retrospect, deep down inside I was concerned about what quick success in the film industry might do to my life and to my marriage. I loved Cristina so much and committed myself first and foremost to making our life work especially once she discovered she had gotten pregnant. So while the film career would be put on hold for a while, Cristina and I had our first son James, born in New York just before we left in 1992. While we faced our own demons like most couples do, each day my relationship with Cristina would grow stronger as we faced both good times and hardships together. Our second son Max would be born in 1998.

I continue working to be the very best husband and father that I can. Although there were times when I've taken a step backwards, I have always managed to take two steps forward. The bottom line always is the sum total of whether you are advancing or moving backwards. It is impossible to stand still since time does not.

As earlier described, in 1991 the Nichiren Shoshu priesthood and the lay organization of Soka Gakkai would part ways. The name NSA (Nichiren Shoshu of America) would be changed to SGI-USA (Soka Gakkai International – USA). The organization would also start taking an approach to its activities that would be more suitable to American culture or the diversification thereof. We would no longer see "street proselytizing" as they had once done in war torn 1947 Japan and the proper use of English words where Japanese words were no longer necessary. While I never considered the organization a "cult" in the classic or stereotypical sense of the word, they had certainly teetered on cultish things because of the foreign culture from Japan that had infused into the American organization. Soka University and the general Soka school system, one of the best in Japan and supported mainly by Soka Gakkai, would also open an outstanding and highly regarded new university in Aliso Viejo, CA; Soka University of America.

Although I would have many more incredible experiences with my Buddhist practice that could fill another book (no hint intended), I knew that everything I was experiencing was part of the journey to my own happiness and which always continues.

Nothing was easy. Nothing has ever been easy. Life is not easy. We would like it to be that way but ease is not synonymous with fulfillment. This is however (for many of us) part of the heaven we hope will greet us following death. How many of us yearn for a place where we will no longer experience unhappiness and where sorrow is non-existent for all eternity? Sounds inviting.

For me however, I cannot imagine anything better than a life fulfilled. I can't imagine anything better than the feeling of loving someone or being loved by another, the challenges of succeeding, the birth of a child, the wonder of a mother's love, the smell of spring rain, that first crush, the time spent with good friends…

the sharing of human artistic expression, or the beauty of culture. These are the things worth fighting for and the stuff that makes life rather than death the place where we can experience ultimate joy. But a place where there is no pain and where you are happy for all eternity? If that is the case, then heaven sounds like hell to me and I share no yearning for such an outcome. Is there any point in that world where I would forget what happiness really is?

If you thought when I said "indestructible" happiness I meant "forever" happiness you would be mistaken. They are not the same. Indestructible means something that can't be taken away from you. Forever means something that never changes. Change is one of the great joys of living and not something to fear but rather something we should embrace. Nor would I say that we need to look any further than this world to find hell while we still have war, ignorance, abuse, meaningless death, and prejudice.

The Ideal of Unity

Unity is a universally accepted ideal that through the ages has displayed its significance in whether something can be accomplished or not. We see this in all aspects of life whether in business, families, and particularly evident in war. The birth of our nation occurred mainly because our founding fathers and American Revolutionary armies were so united in their cause for freedom and independence while the British soldier probably couldn't think of any place he would rather *not* be at that time. Instead his thoughts were back at home in England with his wife and the children he left behind to fight a war for a king's desire that meant very little to his own welfare. But we've also been on the other side of this fight like in Vietnam and which should also be a very certain concern in our machinations in the Middle East.

Many in body and one in mind (*itai doshin*) is the principle concept whereby the goal or ideal of a group is clear and becomes its principle foundation for being. The opposite of that (*dotai ishin* or many in mind but one in body), may be a single group of many but where the goals or ideals of the group are not commonly shared or may even be confused.

I don't think it is incorrect to say that as a human race we have common longings that are non-political, neither liberal or conservative in nature, or need any sort of religious affiliation. We want a peaceful society and peaceful communities. We want a world where our children can grow up safely and never know hunger. We don't want crime. We don't want to be cheated or lied to by our government. We want a world where war is no longer in existence. We would like more harmony with our environment and the eco-systems that support life on our planet.   And in short, we all want a place where we can pursue happiness and fulfillment in our lives.

In spite of all our humane endeavors and kind theoretical intention of our religions, we continue to fail in bringing about a world that befits our existence. Not that we can be faulted for not trying. Goodness knows we constantly try.

How then can we as humans finally realize our own united ultimate goal? Not that it must be through Buddhism or any one religion, but unless we all find our "place" in the ocean of life and become inseparable from it, then we as a species can never hope to achieve the great peace on Earth that we all deeply desire.

"If the spirit of many in body but one in mind prevails among the people, they will achieve all their goals, whereas if one in body but many in mind, they can achieve nothing remarkable." [22]

Kosen-rufu: Rethinking the "World Peace" Process

I'm about to make a statement that will perhaps make more sense than anything I've said to this point and saved it for the last part of this book. *The ideal world and society we all seek can only be achieved through the happiness and peace of each individual person; one person at a time, one community at a time, one country at a time, and then the entire human race as a whole.* This concept is embodied in the ideal we call *Kosen-rufu* and is at the heart of Nichiren's philosophy and his very purpose. It is the culmination of everything that belongs to each person. It is the right and responsibility to live a life of true happiness rather than

---

[22] The Writings of Nichiren Daishonin, Vol. I page 618 (Many in Body, One in Mind)

one that is relative. We won't stop the horrors we wield upon each other both big and small until we lift the veils of illusion and begin living our lives as true human beings since we are the only creatures on the planet that are not really certain what that really means. Birds may know the way of birds, and a fish may know the way of a fish, but does a human being know the way of a human being? If we did our world would be far different than it is now.

Kosen-rufu is a concept that goes far deeper than simply what one might consider "world peace." It is totally and completely focused on the treasure of a single human life and the ability for that life to find true freedom. I am an American free to choose. Free to achieve my highest potential. Free to live where I would like. But my real freedom is that which is expressed in the Declaration of Independence; the right to the pursuit of happiness. I know now that this freedom is not one that is granted to me by any government nor can it ever be taken away. This is because real freedom can be found anywhere. True freedom is one that comes from something within. Freedom from a mind that fears death and freedom from any illusion that happiness is dependent on how much of this or that I might possess. Freedom is found in knowing that there is no person of any religious or governmental authority capable of standing between me and the ultimate benefit of my faith. Freedom is found in the realization that the greatest happiness of all is that which I can share with others.

As mentioned, this book has been dedicated to my father Raymond and most certainly my mother Stella without whom this book would not be possible. And hardly worthy of my presence in her life, this book is belongs to my wife Cristina whose friendship, love, and support is my great and humbling fortune.

www.ingramcontent.com/pod-product-compliance
Lightning Source LLC
Chambersburg PA
CBHW031149270326
41931CB00006B/202